FRESH EXPRESSIONS
IN A DIGITAL AGE

Praise for *Fresh Expressions in a Digital Age*

"The church must engage with culture, and culture continually changes. There are no longer two separate cultural worlds: the flesh and blood, or 'real' world, and the 'virtual' or digital one, but one integrated culture in which the digital shapes the flesh and blood world at least as much as the reverse. An incarnational approach to mission like fresh expressions, where context is the key to planting, must engage the virtual world. The alternative is an aging church that has no place for digital natives. I warmly recommend Michael and Rosario's book. It will show you why this is so, how everyday local churches can take the opportunities offered, and how to avoid the dangers that come with any changed cultural landscape. This is a key read as we (hopefully) emerge from the COVID-19 pandemic with new tools for mission."

—Graham Cray, bishop, chair of the "Mission-Shaped Church" working party, and former Team Leader for Fresh Expressions UK

"This book by my friends Michael and Roz is simply packed with the blend of missional wisdom, innovative ideas, and adaptive possibilities that we need right now. It's just what Dr. Jesus ordered for the ailing church of our times."

—Alan Hirsch, award-winning author of numerous books in missional leadership, organization, and spirituality; founder of Movement Leaders Collective and Forge Missional Training Network

"Recent circumstances have forced churches everywhere to confront what has been a reality for some time: the digital world is a space where life is increasingly unfolding and the church is called to be present. This book by two wise and reflective ministry leaders explores critically what faithful, innovative ministry looks like in a digital age. It is full of concrete stories and practical steps about how the church can navigate the challenges and opportunities of the digital world."

—Dwight Zscheile, Vice President of Innovation and Associate Professor of Congregational Mission and Leadership, Luther Seminary, St. Paul, MN

"Any church leader who is serious about actively living into our present and future reality will find this book a 'must-read.' The authors offer many creative examples of what's possible, 'App It' questions for a team to unpack, plus the strategic new 'E-haviors' to adopt. These are only a few of the user-friendly features that will definitely put your ministry on a new, exciting, multiplying course for Christ."

—Sue Nilson Kibbey, director, Bruce Ough Innovation Center, United Theological Seminary, Dayton, OH

"Wow, this is a thrilling ride of a book. Hold on as you zoom through our context of the digital norm while passing by the COVID-19 pandemic. Now at high speed you will see the vista of what it means to be missionaries today. So not last

year but what it means to be the sent people of God in the present, today, right now. And Michael and Rosario act as our guides and companions for this crazy journey, helping to make sense of what we are seeing and experiencing."
—Dave Male, Director of Evangelism and Discipleship, Church of England

"In a season of accelerated change, the faithful church adapts its methods while remaining clear about purpose—to announce the good news of Jesus and to be his body. A blended ecology will necessarily include a more prominent attention to digital life and spiritual practices that inhabit that space. Michael Beck and Rosario Picardo orient us to the missionary work that awaits us with depth, encouragement, and creativity. This is where we are, and where we are headed!"
—Ken Carter, bishop, Florida Conference, The United Methodist Church

"Every page of *Fresh Expressions in a Digital Age* is filled with many breaths of fresh air and fresh life for all churches, whether fretful or fragrant or funky. Michael and Rosario are both scholar-practitioners who practice what they prescribe. They are guides for a church living on the edge of the future. This resource will help your team follow them to the fault lines."
—Leonard Sweet, best-selling author (*Rings of Fire*), professor, semiotician, and founder of SpiritVenture Ministries, The Salish Sea Press, and www.preachthestory.com

"Roz and Michael have written the book that church leaders need for this time in history. It will give you hope if you have been discouraged. It will empower you to dream again. It provides practical counsel on how to reach people, right now. Simply, it will inspire you to keep going. That's what it did for me. Read this book!"
—Jacob Armstrong, pastor, Providence Church; author, *God's Messy Family, A New Playlist*, and *The New Adapters*

"Pastors Beck and Picardo have done something here that was much needed. This book is very practical with its downloads, applications, and success stories. The digital age is here to stay, and the church has so much to look forward to. It is clear that as prophetic people we must look to the future always. To look back is detrimental and salty. Thank you, pastors, for your insight!"
—Dee Stokes, author, spiritual advisor, coach, speaker, and educator

"Michael and Roz skillfully wrote and compiled a resource to help church leaders navigate the digital age and fulfill the 'Great Commission' in uncertain times. With this resource, you will be ready to lead effectively in the present and the future. A must-read for leaders in the digital age."
—Olu Brown, lead pastor, Impact Church

"*Fresh Expressions in a Digital Age* is written by two excellent practitioners who mash up their ministry experiences in both Fresh Expressions and the emerging digital ministry age. Picardo, Beck, and other guests offer many tools in this invaluable resource to help you fast-track your digital ministry approach. This book will be a must in any ministry leader's toolbox."

—Brad Aycock, director, New Church Development, West Ohio Conference, The United Methodist Church

"This is the helpful resource that all church leaders have been waiting for since the global COVID-19 pandemic turned our world upside down starting in March 2020. I thank God for the leadership of Dr. Michael Beck and Dr. Rosario Picardo as they share the many creative ways they have developed Fresh Expressions of ministry and led their own congregations to greater faithfulness and fruitfulness. They have also brought together nine other outstanding young Christian leaders from all over the nation who demonstrate how congregations can make new disciples of Jesus Christ in creative, innovative, visionary, and authentic ways when people have to shelter in place. In this book, local church pastors and lay leaders will find an abundance of new ideas on how to preach, teach, pastor, and serve their communities and congregations. Read it, discuss it, and share it with your friends."

—Kent Millard, president, United Theological Seminary

Michael Adam Beck
and
Rosario Picardo

FRESH EXPRESSIONS
IN A DIGITAL AGE

How the Church Can Prepare

for a Post-Pandemic World

Nashville

FRESH EXPRESSIONS IN A DIGITAL AGE:
HOW THE CHURCH CAN PREPARE FOR A POST-PANDEMIC WORLD

Library of Congress Control Number: 2021939405

ISBN: 9781791023843

21 22 23 24 25 26 27 28 29 30—10 9 8 7 6 5 4 3 2 1
MANUFACTURED IN THE UNITED STATES OF AMERICA

Home Screen

Login

This past Sunday, thousands of people across the United States gathered around their screens to watch First Cyberia Church.com. A countdown clock with edgy music led to flashy title pages; moving graphics; and images of young, interracial, hip-looking people popping up on their screens. Cue the lights. The camera pans across the multicultural crowd, as the worship band appears on stage (socially distanced, of course). They play in the perfectly lit space, as room colors adjust to the emotional tone of the songs. The stage effects could give professional music artists a run for their money.

Slipped between the perfectly manicured lyrical slides are suggested ways to connect, or how to download the church's app, or how to give financially. Suddenly the online campus pastor appears on screen and lays out the importance of giving and all the many things the church is doing across the globe. A blockbuster, movie-quality sermon series trailer plays on the massive stage screens. Finally, the teaching pastor emerges on the platform, and the main event is a compelling twenty-minute sermon. The camera cycles through multiple angles, zooming in and out, panning across the crowded room, helping everyone stay glued to their screens at home. The service concludes with an opportunity to accept Jesus as Lord and Savior and to provide personal contact info, so an online pastor can follow up.

Is this how you imagine "online church"? Does it seem to be oddly similar to a polished, high production, stage-show performance? Does it feel like a carefully rehearsed, marketed, and executed self-help convention? If you're a leader in a church, does this even seem intimidating?

We mean no offence to those churches that create these versions of digital worship or the Christians who appreciate them. For most of us reading these words, we even celebrate this type of experience and how it might reach a post-Christian Western culture.

However, an experience like this is completely irrelevant to more than 90 percent of pastors and the churches they lead. Many (if not most) churches don't even have a single full-time staff person, much less an entire staff of people working on websites, marketing, and promotion. We may not even have an organ that is fully functional (the bass pedal is currently stuck at Michael's 140-year-old church), much less a light show, smoke machine, camera crew, or teleprompter.

Indeed, the spectacular version of "online church" is largely inaccessible to most church leaders, and frankly many from emerging generations are increasingly turned off by the polished corporate nature of the show. Is Christian life defined as "consumers of religious deliverables"? In some settings this kind of digital worship and consumer faith does more harm than good to the body of Christ.

Yes, this is one version of "online church," but it's not contextually appropriate for many churches. As we will show later, *authenticity trumps production value.* Being authentically who we are—flaws, tech fails, connection blunders, and all—is the true key. The world is longing for us to be real and transparent, rather than polished and perfect. Owning our unique identity is always more powerful than trying to emulate another congregation.

But there is a way that every church—big or small, conservative or progressive, low tech or high tech, no staff or a colony of staff—can find ways to be the church in the digital age. What if you don't even need lots of staff, fancy websites, or light shows to offer Christ and help people grow in their journeys with Jesus? What if every single Christian has the capacity to be a "church planter" on this new digital frontier? What if we can utilize the cheap-to-free technologies we use every day to form new Christian communities?

Evangelism, discipleship, and church planting are not programs, departments, or the expertise of specialists. They are a singular move of the

Spirit that flows through the life of every Jesus follower. When we do this in community with others, we are the fullness of the "priesthood of all believers." On the digital frontier, the playing field has been leveled. Every believer can play a part in God's ever-expanding kingdom.

Who will redeem the techno-sphere? If it's not followers of Jesus that will brave this new digital ecosystem, who will? However, as we will show, to be a digital missionary one must have both flesh-and-blood feet planted firmly in the analog world.

> THE PROMISE PROPOSED IN THIS BOOK
> IS QUITE SIMPLE:
> ANY CHRISTIAN WITH INTERNET ACCESS
> AND A DEVICE CAN BE A MISSIONARY
> IN THE DIGITAL AGE.

Three Stories

Three parallel stories illustrate what we intend to show. First, one of Kevin's favorite places to be is in the movie theater. He has an app on his iPhone connected to a monthly subscription that allows him to watch as many movies as he likes. Also, he gets a discount on his massive popcorn and soda combo! For Kevin, watching a movie is a spiritual practice. It entails ritual, inspiration, and even a monthly offering from his paycheck.

He wanted to share this passion with others, so he created a website and blog for fellow film connoisseurs. They see the same films and then post about what they liked in the chat feed of Kevin's site. Eventually Kevin invites those who are willing to hang out in a Zoom room and talk about the spirituality they find hidden in the films. He asks the group if next time they meet someone would offer a prayer. After praying together for a while and discussing the spirituality of the films each time they meet, Kevin starts to share a devotional from the Bible along with asking a couple questions. Kevin jokingly says, "I think we have become a church!" and the group decides to name themselves *Cinema and Scriptures*.

Second, Brittany loves Lake Silver Park, just two miles from her house. The park features a walking track that winds through the woods and around the lake, a large playground, exercise stations, a frisbee golf course, and a ramp to drop in canoes and kayaks. She creates a Facebook group called *Lovers of Lake Silver*. She uses her various social-media profiles and invites friends to join. She encourages them to post pictures and comments about some of their favorite spots in the park and some of their favorite things to do.

She creates digital scavenger hunts for her group regulars, where they must find certain landmarks in the park and post pictures. She encourages people in the group to create their own special sites and describe why those locations are important to them. Many times, the posts are spiritual in nature and connected to a specific memory. Brittany creates a Facebook event for her group and invites the community to start meeting together at one of the picnic tables, just to chat about life and spirituality. Their love for the place is what binds them initially, but soon they start to form real and deep relationships.

When COVID-19 struck, the group decided to meet in a Facebook room until it was safe to meet in person. In the comfort of the digital space, people begin to share even more openly about the struggles of quarantine, lost employment, and sick loved ones. They begin to pray for each other and send encouraging Bible verses by text message throughout the week. When they were able to meet again, masked and socially distanced at the park, they continued these spiritual practices more intentionally: prayer, scripture reading, and conversation. A church is forming right where they are.

Third, Kathy was a long-time church member who had a passion for poetry. Her church had been involved with forming multiple, innovative, and new Christian communities throughout the city. This inspired her to form her own group. She used Meetup.com to create a community of people interested in poetry. They swapped some of their favorite poems and reflected together in the community chat. After sharing these ideas digitally, they decided to chip in and rent a room in the community center and held their first gathering of *Poetry with a Purpose*. When they gathered, they had a poetry reading, in which each person got up to take turns reading a favorite poem. Kathy begins every meeting with a Psalm from the Bible, offers a brief reflection, and initiates prayer.

AND . . . The Blended Ecology of Church

While the names and titles have been changed, these are real stories from our contexts. We call these little, new Christian communities, "Fresh Expressions of Church." A fresh expression is a form of church for our changing culture, established primarily for the benefit of those who are not yet part of any church.[1]

We use the language of *analog* and *digital*. These words became more frequent for church folks during the global pandemic of 2020, along with other words such as *unprecedented, pivot,* and *social distancing. Analog* in its current popular usage simply refers to physicality, or an in-person, spatial, reality. This is contrasted with the word *digital*, which uses electronic technology that lacks physical, spatial, or an in-person substance. David Sax writes,

> Digital is the language of computers, the binary code of 1's and 0's, which in endless combinations allow computer hardware and software to communicate and calculate. If something is connected to the Internet, runs with the help of software, or is accessed by a computer, it is digital. Analog is the yin to digital's yang, the day to its night. It doesn't require a computer to function, and most often analog exists in the physical world (as opposed to the virtual one).[2]

Often grouped together are the words *inherited, attractional, gathered,* and *analog* church. Usually these adjectives describe more traditional, in-person forms of church. Sometimes the terms are compared or contrasted with the language of *modern, missional, scattered, digital,* and *fresh expressions* of church. For the most part, the latter are contextual forms of church that reach and serve people currently outside the inherited church.

There are exceptions in this analogy because traditional forms of church can be digital, and fresh expressions of church can be analog. To some degree, every church had to become a "digital" church overnight, when mandatory quarantine precautions came forth. Whether we liked the result or not, if we wanted to have a worship experience on Sunday morning, we had to figure out how to do it digitally.

Distributed simply means "spread" or "shared." We of the Fresh Expressions movement often hold this word in creative tension with the *collected* church. Regardless of the tensive pairings we use—"gathered and scattered," "centered and dispersed," "attractional and missional," "digital and analog"—the key leverage is the word *and*. We advocate here for a blended ecology, where these modes of church live together.

The blended ecology refers to fresh expressions of church in symbiotic relationship with inherited forms of church, in such a way that the combining of these modes over time blend to create a nascent form. Surely, the present future calls for a blended ecology of digital and analog, collected and distributed, gathered and scattered forms of church.

Live from the Digital Frontier!

We write this book together from front-line action in the local church. We apply this experience on different scales and in different practices in the trenches of a digital frontier every week. We are practitioners who reflect critically on the experiments and innovations transforming our life together.

Rosario "Roz" Picardo has served in all facets of church life from a custodian to an executive pastor at a megachurch. His primary call is to be a church planter. Mosaic Church is a three-year-old church that has excelled in both the analog and digital platforms. Since Mosaic has no building and found themselves homeless from their third space (a movie theater) during COVID-19, they decided to become nomads for four months by worshipping drive-in style in different parking lots throughout the Dayton, Ohio, region. To continue their online presence, they brought on an online campus pastor who helps facilitate their online congregation's spiritual growth by shaping a custom service that is a different experience from drive-in worship.

Michael Adam Beck serves as co-pastor of two analog United Methodist congregations with his wife, Jill, where they direct addiction-recovery programs, a jail ministry, a food pantry, an interracial unity movement and house both a faith-based inpatient treatment center and a homeless shelter for men reentering society after prison. Wildwood and St. Marks are traditional congregations and a network of thirteen digital and analog fresh expressions that gather in tattoo parlors, dog parks, salons, running tracks, community centers, burrito joints, Facebook groups, and Zoom rooms.

These inherited and emerging churches are all overseen by teams of "lay" leaders, retired clergy, and a couple candidates exploring ordained ministry. Wildwood has two quarter-time pastors and a very part-time office manager. Saint Mark's shares those two part-time clergy, plus another quarter-time deacon. Both historic congregations were in a tailspin of significant decline spanning decades. Now each week this network of churches is touching the lives of hundreds of people across a whole region through physical, digital, and hybrid forms of church. No one is paid to oversee technology, worship production, outreach, or evangelism—or even to update the websites.

If these churches can use the challenges of the digital age to their advantage to "make disciples of Jesus Christ for the transformation of the world," any church can do this. In this book, we show some practical ways to do it too.

Desperation is the seedbed for innovation. COVID-19 will wreak a lot of havoc for years to come, but Christ-followers respond by loving their neighbors through social distancing, which even broke the internet!

Many churches that have never streamed their services before were forced to do so under strong suggestions and ordinances. The internet is nothing new, but streaming church services is a new wineskin for many congregations as a response to a global pandemic.

Overnight, congregations were forced into the future. The question was: How will the hundreds of nations affected by COVID-19 be any different after this global pandemic? How will the church (like an old dog) learn new skills and new tricks? Will these methods continue to change and evolve as the message is proclaimed in new ways?

But what about congregations who live out their calling primarily in the first space (home), second space (school and work), and third place (neutral or community environments)? How did practitioners of fresh expressions respond? These pioneers lost the very spaces they depend on for forming church with people in the normal rhythms of their daily lives. Many worked with all that was left, the first place: peoples' living rooms. Missional entrepreneurs utilized the space of flows and harnessed the power of digital connectivity to release new forms of church. They, too, have been forced into a new paradigm.

This pandemic triggered urgent theological reflections on "real virtuality," incarnational mission, placefulness, evangelism, disciple formation, worship planning, digital intimacy, and authority concerning sacramental practices. We will explore these challenges in practical ways.

In this field guide, we hope to share best practices to reach as many people as possible, while also being faithful to a church's DNA and context. The implications for engagement transcend traditions, theology, age, political affiliation, and social entertainment. It is our hope that you discover the best ways God has created you to facilitate community best.

Instruction Manual

Here's how this book works . . .

Downloads: Rather than chapter labels, this book has downloads. A download is the act or process of downloading data. We prayerfully downloaded this data from a wide variety of church experiences, and now we're curating it for you to download and use. You are encouraged to digest it, transform it, and offer it to others for download.

App It: Following each Download we offer an "App It" section designed to help with *application* of the principles we cover. Each App It features . . .

- **Chat Box:** Some questions to help your team contextualize the ideas for your own setting.

- **Missional E-haviors:** A list of suggested missional practices and principles connected to the content.

Livestreams: Following each App It section you will find "livestreams." This is a collaborative work. The livestreams are interviews with digital missionaries involved in cultivating the blended ecology of analog and digital at varying levels. We mean "livestreaming" in the sense of broadcasting from an available platform in real time, with practitioners on the missional frontier who are living out the concepts now. It's also significant that "streams" give "life." Nothing gets a congregation's blood pumping again like resurrection stories of lives transformed by Jesus. Many of us learn more through stories than taking in data, so we will offer up both options for you.

The Digital Age

On May 24, 1844, Samuel Morse sent the first telegraph message over a wire stretching the forty miles between Washington, D.C., and Baltimore, Maryland, where his co-inventor and machinist, Alfred Vail, was waiting to receive the telegraph. The historic first message read, "What hath God wrought?" Instantly, Vail responded, "What hath God wrought!"

The word *telegraph* is derived from a Greek word that means "to write far." The first telegraph worked by transmitting electrical signals over a wire laid between stations. This device and its corresponding system allowed the rapid transmission of information by coded signal. Morse and Vail created what came to be known as Morse code. The code assigned letters and numbers a set of dots and dashes, rendered as marks on a piece of paper that the telegraph operator would then translate back into English. The electric telegraph evolved and became the principal means of transmitting printed information by wire or radio wave for over one hundred years.

The telegraph was the defining communication technology of its day, and it revolutionized long-distance communication. This incredible achievement started the telecommunications revolution. This was the first modern technological expression of "distanced contact."

Up until this point, communication primarily required "direct contact" through physical contiguity. While information traveling by horse and ship allowed for distanced communication, it was not rapid. Sociologist Manuel Castells describes distanced contact as "simultaneity introduced in social relationships at a distance."[1] Through the telegraph humans could interact rapidly across great distances.

Samuel Morse was a devoutly religious man, and a strong believer in "manifest destiny," which linked ideas of an American empire with divine providence. Morse saw himself as an instrument of this providence. That first message was dictated to Morse by his friend and daughter of the commissioner of patents, Miss Annie Ellsworth (for whom Samuel had designs). Annie Ellsworth's mother, Nancy, selected this phrase from the King James Version of the book of Numbers: "What hath God wrought" (Num 23:23). This ambition was motivating for members of a young nation, among whom Ralph Waldo Emerson famously proclaimed, "America is the country of the Future. It is a country of beginnings, of projects, of vast designs and expectations."[2]

Numbers 23:23 is nestled in the context of a prophetic interaction between Balak and Balaam about the coming prosperity of Israel:

> God brought them out of Egypt; he hath as it were the strength of a unicorn. Surely there is no enchantment against Jacob, neither is there any divination against Israel: according to this time it shall be said of Jacob and of Israel, What hath God wrought! Behold, the people shall rise up as a great lion, and lift up himself as a young lion: he shall not lie down until he eat of the prey, and drink the blood of the slain. (KJV)

Samuel Morse saw the fledgling nation as a promised land, and a new Israel. Morse said later that this verse "baptized the American Telegraph with the name of its author": God.[3] Morse's motivation typifies the mingling of Christianity and the dominant American synthesis of science and religion of the time. This combination of Protestantism and Enlightenment shaped American culture and institutions.[4]

Consider this excerpt from a Methodist women's magazine describing the role the electric telegraph would have. We can see the mixture of optimism and hubris characteristic of the time:

This noble invention is to be the means of extending civilization, repub-
licanism, and Christianity over the earth. It must and will be extended
to nations half-civilized, and thence to those now savage and barbarous.
Our government will be the grand center of this mighty influence. . . .
The beneficial and harmonious operation of our institutions will be
seen, and similar ones adopted. Christianity must speedily follow them,
and we shall behold the grand spectacle of a whole world, civilized, re-
publican, and Christian.[5]

Perhaps we are seeing a return of this very kind of rhetoric today,
once again fueled by emerging technologies like social media? There is a
grave danger in this kind of Christian syncretism with civil religion. It is
no secret that churches in the United States can function as handmaids
to imperialism, slavery, and the genocide of indigenous peoples—in the
name of progress.

So, we begin this exploration with a word of hopeful caution for the
church. The telegraph truly was a feat of technological ingenuity that enabled new forms of communication and therefore human flourishing.
Christians have often led the way in harnessing the emerging technologies
for the expansion of the faith. Examples include the Roman road and
courier systems of Paul's day, which helped the first scattered churches
communicate and multiply. Another example is the early Christian use
of the codex to preserve and spread the Gospels. Yet another example is
Johannes Guttenberg's printing press, which was used to disseminate the
Bible to everyone and fueled the Reformation. Billy Graham's use of stadiums, microphones, and speakers, which seeded the birth of the first megachurches, is another such use of technology to spread the faith. Christians
have a long history of using emerging technologies in redemptive ways.
The telegraph gave way to the telephone, then to the radio, and then to the
television, each of which helped enable the church to grow and expand.

It would be reckless not to acknowledge right up front the dangers
of using these technologies. As we will show, digital technologies are not
neutral. They can dehumanize us to the point that we become the means
to the ends of corporate profits. In the Digital Age, this phenomenon
has been called the *Attention Economy*. Our attention, our time, and our

resources become the commodity that is being mined. We become the "users," and our lives are reduced to "data."

As with all use of technologies, there are both tremendous benefits and incredible dangers.

Perhaps it is fitting to *begin* this exploration of the Digital Age with the *end*. For Christians, understanding our current context can only be properly done by seeing it through the lens of God's future. The clearest portrait of creation's ultimate destiny is found in the book of Revelation. There we see a universe that started in a garden has finally been transformed into a hybrid garden/city.

> Then the angel showed me the river of the water of life, bright as crystal, flowing from the throne of God and of the Lamb through the middle of the street of the city. On either side of the river is the tree of life with its twelve kinds of fruit, producing its fruit each month; and the leaves of the tree are for the healing of the nations. (Rev 22:1-2)

Humanity was exiled from that first garden through sin, sending all forthcoming human civilization, and creation itself, toward the inevitable curse of death (Gen 3). Following the murder of his brother, Abel, Cain flees to the land of Nod. There he helps build the first city, itself a technological marvel, where various kinds of technology proliferate, including musical instruments as well as the first bronze and iron tools (Gen 4:17-26). The first city seems to be humanity's attempt to use technology to live apart from God (Gen 4). Later we use technology in a similar way: "Come, let us build ourselves a city, and a tower with its top in the heavens, and let us make a name for ourselves" (Gen 11:4). Our ability to use tools and create can lead to pride, and pride always ends in our downfall (Prov 16:18). This has been a repeated pattern of humanity ever since.

Thus it is all the more important to see that our final destination is an integration of all our human technologies—a city—as well as a restored garden and a renewed cosmos stripped free of the curse of death. Our future is a blended ecology. Somehow our greatest creations, made with sin-broken materials, will be redeemed (Rev 21–22). There is redemption not only for what God has made but what we, as reflections of the creator and stewards of that gift, make from it.

Our future is a God-centered community that consists of all the tribes of the earth gathered at the tree of life in a hybrid urban-garden.

Let's consider the prophetic wisdom of Jacques Ellul, French philosopher, sociologist, lay theologian, professor, and notable Christian anarchist. In *Presence in the Modern World*, Ellul reminds us that the role of Christians is neither to separate from or be conformed to the world: "We are to be in it but not of it." Followers of Jesus, embody God's future, one that is breaking into the present:

> Christians stand before humankind, within the world's spiritual reality, as the visible sign of the new covenant that God has made with this world in Jesus Christ. Christians must be a true sign, however: their life and words must manifest this covenant to humankind. Otherwise the earth feels itself bereft of covenant. It no longer knows where it is headed and lacks any possible self-understanding or certainty to its preservation.[6]

Overall, what Jacques called the "technological society" lacks reference to God's promised future, which leads humanity to confuse the "means with the ends." Christians must call into question all that is termed *progress*, discoveries, facts, established results, and so on. In this sense, Christians fulfill a prophetic function as "bearers of the eschaton." Ellul writes, "Science today takes its meaning from technique; it is completely oriented to application. It is in service of means."[7]

Everything has become means, including humankind ourselves. The end no longer exists. The underlying myth is that people must be happy, which is achieved through consuming goods and services, enabled through technological advancements with more and more ease. That "the ends justify the means" is no longer valid. Today the means is whatever succeeds, whatever is efficacious. If it is effective, it is justified in the name of progress, and "if the church no longer seems relevant in the world, it's because of the new situation of the problem of means."[8]

Ellul shows how even the spiritual has been placed in the service of means. Religion itself becomes a transaction between producer and consumer. We pay our tithes and receive our religious goods and services. We draw up strategic plans, programs, and the means of actions to get our results. This is mere imitation of the world, not bearing God's promised future in the present. Ellul argues it is the expression of the Holy Spirit working within us and being expressed in our material life through words, habits, and decisions that is truly revolutionary. This is ultimately a matter of being and not doing. Change comes through the church's faith and not from the technical competence of specialists.

We cannot transform the world through effort or activity, but through union with Christ, we can be a microcosm of God's future, living in the present. The church then lives in an unresolvable dialectical tension with the world. Ultimately the healing and transformation of the world will only be completed with Jesus' triumphant return. So, new Christian communities, filled with the Holy Spirt, living the way of Jesus, could be the "seeds of a new civilization" that may spring up from the soils of God's future.[9]

As we launch into this exploration of the digital age, we do so from this fundamental premise: *being a faithful witness for Christ in the digital frontier requires critical examination of technology and its underlying assumptions.*

How do we offer *faithful presence* in the digital ecosystem, participate in it but not be of it? How do we hold in critical tension the capacity to analyze modern technology and be missionaries within it, embodying God's revealed future now? How do we be God's *ends* in a world of *means*?

"What Hath God Wrought?"

We find ourselves in another "communications revolution" moment in world history. The telecommunications movement that kicked off with the telegraph in 1844 led to the invention of the telephone in 1876. The basic structures of the internet were being developed as early as 1962. Advanced Research Projects Agency Network (ARPANET) was the first wide-area packet-switching network to come online in 1969. Email came along in in 1971, the first global networking started in 1973, the first public internet in 1974, the World Wide Web in 1991, and the portable internet in 1996.

This global system of interconnected computer networks and devices now spans private, public, academic, business, and government connectivity. It has enabled the first truly global human community, linked by a broad array of electronic, wireless, and optical networking technologies. The internet is a massive expanse of information resources and services, including inter-linked hypertext documents and server applications hosted in the cloud, electronic mail, telephony, and file sharing.

This communication revolution not only revolutionized how we communicate; it changes how human beings think, work, fall in love, and live.

Canadian philosopher, and technological prophet Marshall McLuhan (1911–1980) first said "the medium is the message." McLuhan has been called the founder of the academic discipline of "media ecology" (the study of information environments). He proposed that the medium itself shaped and controlled "the scale and form of human association and action."[10] He was the first to advocate that a communication medium itself, not the messages it carries, should be the primary focus of study. He showed that a technology widely used in society changes the content and characteristics of that society. The effects of technology go deep; the medium shapes our very patterns of sensation and perception. McLuhan writes:

> Now, in the electric age, the very instantaneous nature of co-existence among our technological instruments has created a crisis quite new in human history. Our extended faculties and senses now constitute a single field of experience which demands that they become collectively conscious. Our technologies, like our private senses, now demand an interplay and ratio that makes rational co-existence possible. As long as our technologies were as slow as the wheel or the alphabet or money, the fact that they were separate, closed systems was socially and psychically supportable. This is not true now when sight and sound and movement are simultaneous and global in extent.[11]

McLuhan believed that "When technology extends one of our senses, a new translation of culture occurs as swiftly as the new technology is interiorized." So, a theory of cultural change is not possible without knowledge of the "changing sense ratios effected by various externalizations of our senses" through these technologies. He believed culture to be a "mechanical fate for societies, the automatic interiorization of their own technologies."[12]

In *Tools and Weapons: The Promise and Peril of the Digital Age*, Brad Smith, President and chief legal officer at Microsoft, writes,

> More and more, we find ourselves absorbed in electronic conversations with people we aren't physically with. Sometimes we are a world apart. Digital technology has made the world smaller—and people more accessible—but it has also cast a deafening silence between people sitting next to each other. This phenomenon is nothing new. For more than a century, almost every technology that has connected people who live apart has also created new barriers between people who live close together.[13]

Smith shows that, in the 1960s, landline telephones both connected and separated families. Teenagers retreated to their bedrooms to spend time with their friends on the phone, and later this same behavior was true for computer use. Families found themselves "alone together" in the same home. Today, smartphones allow kids to be in closer physical proximity with their parents, but many times their minds are somewhere else. Thus, many families develop a policy for "no phones at the supper table." While technology makes the world smaller and more integrated globally, people are often less connected with the neighbors next door or family under the same roof.[14]

Nevertheless, the past several decades can be defined as a time of techno-optimism. We assumed these emerging technologies would determine the development of social structures and cultural values positively. As we have seen since the telegraph and Morse code, this ideology has a long history in American political culture. In one respect, the seeds planted in Morse's day sprouted as a new religion with slight Christian undertones. Faith in a crucified savior on a cross was replaced with faith in the god of American ingenuity and technological progress.

There is no question that digital computing and communication are forces for massive good. Technology is used to cure disease, restore blindness, and replace organs. We use these technologies to analyze history more accurately, predict natural disasters, purify water, and pursue new strategies to heal a sick planet. Technology will potentially allow us to establish the first colony on Mars, and for the first time in history, make humanity a multi-planetary species. We can connect across space and time, utilizing the collective intelligence of the entirety of human civilization to connect, collaborate, and solve emerging challenges. McLuhan envisioned that technology would create a "Global Village" twenty years before it materialized. The web has indeed enabled that vision, allowing us to be informed and empowered global citizens.

Claude Shannon, American mathematician, electrical engineer, and cryptographer has been called the architect of the Information Age and "father of information theory." Shannon introduced the notion of a "bit" in a seventy-nine-page monograph for *The Bell System Technical Journal,* titled "A Mathematical Theory of Communication." The bit was a new fundamental unit of measure according to Shannon, "a unit for measuring information." Shannon's theory influenced computing, genetics, neuroscience, and artificial intelligence. Shannon's work on "information theory" catalyzed the sensemaking framework of modern consciousness, which now undergirds the digital age.[15]

Missionaries on a Digital Frontier

What does this mean for Christians? The convergence of these technologies enables the most connected generation of humanity in world history. Human beings were created for relationship with God and with each other. Relationships require connection, time, and communication. As followers of Jesus we find ourselves on a new frontier, and we need to consider how these technologies can be used for missional fruitfulness.

Can we use internet technology as a tool to facilitate community? Can we form real, authentic relationships through this medium? John Dyer writes:

On the surface, all an analog phone does is transport speech from here to there. But if we think differently about what's happening, the phone is transforming the physical world by connecting two people who are physically distant. In addition, the presence of a smart cell phone in my pocket means that my conceptions of space, time, and limits, are radically different than a world without cell phones.[16]

The invention of language helped humanity communicate and share ideas, dreams, and needs. The invention of libraries gave us a place to store and access the accumulation of those communications. The more rapidly and clearly we can communicate, the more we can share knowledge. In many ways, we have never been so connected, with so many, so easily, and in so many places. We can communicate instantaneously across previously segregated cultures.

Technology creates new social conventions, and sometimes technology will create a new way to experience older social conventions. For instance, Christians have been singing together since Jesus sung with his disciples in the upper room (Matt 26:30). For centuries hymnals and songbooks were used in corporate worship. Yet the creation of the projector transformed how Christians sang together. About half the churches embraced this emerging technology, installing screens in the sanctuary. Now rather than lowering our heads to read the lines of a hymnal, we look forward to the slides projected before us. In many churches hymnals now sit unused in the pew or are removed completely. However, prior to the pandemic in 2019, about two-thirds of churches said they prefer print songbooks and half of these want print as well as screens.[17] The shift to this technology comes with some worship conflict!

Technology is not simply produced by human culture; technology reshapes human culture itself in positive and negative ways. Computers are not "just tools" because we are shaped by our tools. Genesis 4 doesn't tell us specifically *what* Cain used to slay his brother, Able. However, there is an interesting interpretation in the book of Jasher, a non-canonical scroll referenced in Joshua, Samuel, and Kings that states, "And Cain hastened and rose up, and took the iron part of his ploughing instrument, with which he suddenly smote his brother and he slew him, and Cain spilt the blood of his brother Abel upon the earth, and the blood of Abel streamed upon the earth before the flock" (Jasher 1:25). Ever since Cain used a tool in the field to kill his brother, humans have been using their tools as weapons.

You can use wood and nails to build a house or to crucify the savior of the world.

Kevin Kelly discusses the internet fostering a new form of "digital socialism," which makes possible a global collaboration never seen before in human history. The values of this digitally connected community include sharing, cooperation, collaboration, and collectivism—all unleashed through e-haviors like networking, tagging, crowdsourcing, remixing, archiving, and rating. Some advancements occur through simply remixing older technologies. This re-appropriation and reuse of existing technology, coupled with sharing, is distressing the traditional understandings of property. Anti-libertarians think this could eventually disrupt the current capitalist system by challenging foundational concepts like *property ownership* itself.[18]

In the cyberia of global collaboration, interconnected webs of microcommunities are transforming the meaning of community. People who may have never met physically are connecting across geographies around shared interests, passions, and hobbies.

Marilee Sprenger, the "brain lady," is an international educational consultant in the fields of social-emotional learning, literacy, vocabulary, and brain research. In *Brain-Based Teaching in the Digital Age* Sprenger writes, "We need to use the technology tools, learn the digital dialogue, and understand and relate better to our students. The key to learning is relationships. Many of our students have strong relationship with and through these digital devices."[19]

As followers of Jesus we believe the key to *everything* is relationships. Our very spiritual, physical, emotional existence is connected to our ongoing relationship with Jesus and each other, apart from those relationships there is no life (John 15:5). Technology enables connection, communication, and relationships in powerful and real ways.

11

Yet we know that the benefits of these technologies are not distributed evenly, and that these same technologies are used in malicious ways. Jenny Odell writes, "Platforms such as Facebook and Instagram act like dams that capitalize on our natural interest in others and an ageless need for community, hijacking and frustrating our most innate desires, and profiting from them."[20] Fake news, the monetization of attention, screen fatigue, and social media addiction are creating a generation prone to anxiety, low self-esteem, and suicide. Neuroscientist Susan Greenfield shows that our digital habits are rewiring the chemical landscape of our brains, in ways just as damaging as compulsive engagement in rewarding stimuli despite adverse consequences.[21]

McLuhan wrote prophetically, "This is merely to say that the personal and social consequences of any medium—that is, of any extension of ourselves—result from the new scale that is introduced into our affairs by each extension of ourselves, or by any new technology." He went on to argue that any technology contrived and experimented with by humans "has the power to numb human awareness during the period of its first interiorization."[22] While technology is making us smarter in many ways, our reliance upon it is also making us dumber in others.

Sprenger's research shows that attention capacity is diminished by spending time immersed in technology in the digital realm. Online gratification releases dopamine in the brain. The neural pathways for addiction to technology are the same as to drugs, but it's unlikely that "abstinence" will be a viable option from technology. It's easy to get lost in cyberspace. Screens provide the potential to form in-person relationships, but the brain craves social-physical interaction. While face-to-face relationships are not *required* in the digital age, we need to work hard to sustain those kinds of interactions in our lives.[23]

The good news from research in neuroscience is that the brain has a high degree of plasticity (i.e., the quality of being easily shaped or molded) or, in this case, *re*shaped and *re*molded. It's never too late to change digital habits. In the following sections we will suggest activities that require sustained attention to rebuild those parts of the brain that are often diminished by engagement with digital technologies. We will also suggest some simple ways to sustain in-person relationships.

The optimism around the World Wide Web has been eroding for the past decade.

Brad Smith writes, "Some say that data has become the oil of the twenty-first century."[24] Indeed, every aspect of our day-to-day lives is fueled by data, much like the Industrial Age was fueled by oil. Yet in the attention economy, we have become the primary target of the capitalist system. Our attention is monetized on digital platforms, so third-party companies can try to sell us their products. In a sense, *we have become the products* for big tech companies. We are the data that is being harvested.

Most church leaders are apprehensive in understanding and engaging this emerging technological reality. Rightfully so. It's scary and dangerous stuff. However, the church itself utilizes multiple layers of technology that would have been considered strange or even idolatrous to generations past. It is hypocritical to judge emerging technology while gripping tightly to our own. Understanding the technology of a new generation, as well as the technology of our own inheritance, is a much-needed expression of contextual intelligence.

John Dyer wisely says, "When technology has distracted us to the point that we no longer examine it, it gains the greatest opportunity to enslave us."[25]

As we explore what it means to faithfully follow Jesus in our time we need to understand the new digital frontier where we find ourselves. Is the technology of the digital age a tool? Yes. Is the technology of the digital age a weapon? Yes. It is both/and. Can we use these technologies to share the gospel and form new Christian communities? The answer is not only yes, but also that we *must* discover how to do so.

Yet what we propose in this book is not merely that technology is a tool or weapon but that the amalgamation of these technologies creates a new kind of space. Digitization has created a new missional frontier. This new ecosystem must be explored on its own terms, through an incarnational posture. This is more than just streaming church services. That can become a new form of colonialism: invading a space we have not been invited, using language only we understand, attempting to conform people to our customs, rather than listening, loving, and building relationships.

Further, we are newcomers to this frontier. For many groups, like the disabilities community for example, their only form of community has been digital for over a decade. People who experience similar disabilities that limit interaction in the physical environment interact directly and freely with others across the globe in the digital environment. The internet provides them a whole new world of possibility in which they live their online lives as people without disabilities if they so choose. It offers new ways to pursue employment, education, and relationships. Online life is life. They are natives here, and we are guests, and there is much to learn.

Manuel Castells describes the emerging social structure of the digital age as the network society. The network society consists of a social structure made up of networks enabled by microelectronics-based information and communications technologies.[26] At the simplest level, a network is a set of interconnected nodes. So, these networks of technologically enabled flows of multimodal communication connect in real physical and digital localities that Castells calls "nodes."

In a network society, we must now recognize the difference between two kinds of space: the *space of place* and the *space of flows*. Castells believes that space throughout human history has been "the material support of simultaneity in social practice." So, cities, for instance, are communication systems, increasing the chance of communication through physical contiguity (direct contact). He calls the *space of place* the space of contiguity.[27] The internet, along with computerized transportation, creates the possibility of simultaneity introduced in social relationships at a distance (again distanced contact). This means that humans no longer need to interact face-to-face in a physical place to have "contact." This transformation of the spatiality of social interaction through simultaneity creates a new kind of space: *the space of flows*. Castells defines the space of flows as "the material support of simultaneous social practices communicated at a distance."[28]

Microelectronic and communication technologies serve as *flows* that enable us to connect across geographies and time. "Flows" of capital, information, organizational interaction, images, sounds, and symbols move along a complex web of interconnected networks enabled by these technologies. Flows are the means through which the movement of people, objects, and things is accomplished from one node to another in social space. The network society is an interconnected matrix, activated by these technologically-enabled flows. The flows are the social organization, the expression of processes dominating our economic, political, and symbolic life.[29]

So, in the same way that cities provided opportunities for encounters in the space of continuity, the digital ecosystem facilitates distanced contact in the space of flows. A city is a built environment that both facilitates and limits the movement of people through a space. The web is similar to a city; it is a digitally built environment that facilitates and limits the movement of people through a virtual ecosystem. Connections, passions, and relationships are all formed in the built environment of a city and are equally facilitated with others in the cyberscape.

This forces us to reconsider fundamentally some assumptions about the digital environment. The web and wireless communications are more than traditional media; they are a global means of interactive, multimodal, and mass self-communication. Castells writes,

> For hundreds of millions of Internet users under 30, on-line communities have become a fundamental dimension of everyday life that keeps growing everywhere . . . on-line communities are fast developing not as a virtual world, but as a real virtuality integrated with other forms of interaction in an increasingly hybridized everyday life.[30]

To say then that "virtual" is in some sense less "real" is a missional cul-de-sac. For many, the virtual space is no more or less real than the physical space that their bodies inhabit. For digital natives (those born with screens in their homes) social networks, such as Facebook, Twitter, and Pinterest, MySpace, Second Life, and Friendster, constitute a very real part of their lives.

When the COVID-19 pandemic forced mandatory stay-at-home orders, was the online worship offered by churches not real? When we attended the funerals of loved ones digitally, was it somehow less real? When we communicated by FaceTime with loved ones locked down in care facilities, were our interactions fake?

Timothy Luke, building on the work of Castells, shows that cyberspace is an expression of the nodes, hubs, and flows of the network. In other words, the digital space of bits and bytes is the result of the "machinic infrastructure of boxes and wires, cables and satellites, servers and relays that anchor the built networks, which, in turn, generate such new, hyperreal electronic environments."[31]

Luke refers to cyberspace as a meta-territorial, and meta-national, domain. The meta-nation of cyberspace "is inside of each nation, but also outside of it; for each nation, but also not for it; by each nation, but also not of it." In this space, face-to-face interactions between persons become online events with digital beings. Currently, the digital venue mainly supplements offline practices, but increasingly face-to-face practices will be supplanted by online alternatives. Luke states, "Eventually, networks will entirely displace many off-line practices with e-structures and that need very little territorial legitimation or personal authentication off-line. It is in these quadrants of change that e-publican ideologies and movements develop."[32]

Luke shows that cyberspace is more than mere clusters of code experienced as audio, graphics, text, or video out on the network. But, rather, that "these digital objects constitute portals into the experience of new types of community, work, identity, sex, utility, knowledge, or power in e-public forms of life." He writes of the "Meganet" as

> a powerful but enigmatic engine of change, the biggest and most complex machine in human history. Its effects are paradoxically universal and parochial, uniting and dividing, constructive and destructive. It will create a new communications culture, overlaid on old ethnic, economic, religious, and national patterns and attitudes. An electronic environment is evolving in which old guideposts are submerged in a stream of bits and bytes exchanging a bewildering variety of messages among billions of individuals.[33]

In short, the network is the machinery that creates the web, enabling a new form of space, time, and in a sense a new global nation. It is a world that transcends the world. It is the infrastructure for what has been called the digital age.

The digital age is simply the time period starting in the late 1970s when the personal computer became available. In the 1980s, computer access combined with the internet in the 1990s facilitated the dramatic proliferation of digital devices. In the 2010s, the smartphone revolution, essentially placed a supercomputer into the pocket of billions of human beings, creating a new social web and hyper-connected mobile technology. It's also called the Information Age because the emerging computer technologies created the capacity to collect and transfer information freely and rapidly. Again, *data* is the "new oil" powering the machine of progress. The broader usage of these technologies within society became the driving force of social evolution.

Let's pause and think of the magnitude of the size of this global cyberspace:

- In 1996, 16 million people were using the internet (0.4 percent of the global population).

- Almost 4.57 billion people were active internet users as of July 2020 (encompassing 59 percent of the global population of 7.8 billion).

- From 2000 to 2019, internet usage increased 1,157 percent.

- Within America, 89.4 percent of people uses the internet daily; in Europe, 87.7 percent uses the internet daily.

- In 2019, 51.5 percent of all internet traffic worldwide was conducted on mobile devices.

- Facebook has 2.414 billion active users.

- Instagram has 1.3 billion active users.

- Twitter has 330 million active users.

- YouTube has 1.8 billion unique monthly visitors.

- Netflix has 150 million unique monthly visitors.

- Sixty-eight percent of Americans use Facebook as their primary social media channel.

- In 2018, global ecommerce (online stores) totaled 653 billion US dollars in sales.

- Ninety-six percent of Americans shop online.[34]

- The average American adult spends 5.4 hours a day on their smartphone.

- Millennials spend an average of 5.7 hours, each day, on their phones; baby boomers spend an average of five hours per day. (However, a larger percentage of baby boomers than millennials spend an excess of twelve hours of screen time each day.)[35]

Just think about the fact that Facebook became the largest nation on the earth back in 2016. The digital space is inhabited by the largest human population in the history of civilization. It is by far the most enormous mission field *ever*.

We encourage you to become missionaries on this new frontier. Yes, all mission fields are dangerous. Many missionaries were killed across history. Digital culture too has its own dangers, which we will explore.

Each maturing generation struggles to embrace the technology of emerging generations. We need to know we have this bias. We can too easily cast stones at new technologies, while not realizing that language, clothing, books, writing paper, pen, ink, and automobiles are all technologies many of use gratefully every day.

McLuhan preferred to use the term *interiorization* to describe our use of technology. This describes the often-unconscious process of how we incorporate the tools we bring into our inner lives. We use layers of technology accumulating across the span of human civilization. These technological amalgamations create and shape our culture, and rarely are we introspective about their use. Yet when new technologies emerge, often we are instinctively resistant.

However, if you are reading this you are already a netizen of cyberia. You are reading a book that's first edition started as an e-book, an innovation in its own right of the digital age. You most likely communicate daily by emails, FaceTime, or Zoom with loved ones. You also may likely receive your paycheck digitally through electronic deposit and then spend it digitally on Amazon, PayPal, ecommerce sites, or the website of your favorite major department store. You already exist, in a sense, in the digital world. Most of us now have virtual lives as well as physical ones.

The web could be thought of as one massive, global city where one may encounter netizens from anywhere in the world. One can leverage this relational access to people across the globe, without losing a sense of connection to the physical location, the access point. Later we will suggest some ways those two spaces can be engaged equally.

Sprenger shows that currently in the information age we are either a "digital native" or a "digital immigrant." She describes those born between 1965 and 1976 as Generation X (typified by high education levels, i.e., *digital immigrants*), those born between 1977 and 1998 Generation Y (the net generation or "net gens," those who grew up using computers, i.e., *digital natives*), and finally those born after 1999 as Generation Z (*digital natives* at birth).[36] She shows that digital natives actually acquire information differently, using the distinction "icon vs. text." Those who grew up accessing information in the Guttenberg age do so through reading lines of text from left to right, top to bottom. Those who grew up in the digital age access and process information primarily through interpreting iconic symbols.[37]

As digital natives ourselves, we realize that what we suggest here will be more challenging for digital immigrants. At the very least, contextual intelligence in the digital age requires a new question: What technology is connecting these people? So, later we will suggest a process of triple listening: to God, to the physical space, and to the digital space. Missionaries need to use all three modes.

Let the adventure of faithfully following Jesus in the digital age now begin!

App It (Application)

Chat Box

Gather with your team physically or digitally and discuss the following questions.

1. Discuss the difference between analog and digital forms of church. Which does each person prefer and why?

2. What technologies do your analog forms of church use regularly? (E.g., hymnals, pews, projector, musical instruments, Power-Point, and so on.) Think critically about these technologies. In what ways are they "tools"; in what ways are they "weapons"?

3. What technologies do your digital forms of church use regularly? (E.g., social media, a website, online giving, programming, live stream, YouTube, and so on.) Think critically about these technologies. In what ways are they "tools"; in what ways are they "weapons"?

4. How have the various technologies discussed by the authors enhanced society? In what ways have they harmed it?

5. In what ways have you seen the church change in response to the digital age? Name both positives and negatives.

E-haviors

Consider how these practices might be helpful as missionaries in the digital age.

Network Inventory

Networking: A network is simply a system of interconnected people or things. The internet is a global network that itself connects a multitude of micro-networks. This allows us to interact with others to exchange information and develop social contacts around common interests or goals. The greatest place to start networking flows from our own passions, hobbies, or causes. Create a "Network Inventory" using the following format.

Simply make a list for each question:

1. What are my favorite things to do?
2. Where do I do them?
3. What causes am I passionate about?
4. Who else do I know who shares these interests?
5. What technologies do people use to connect around these practices?
6. How might I join into an existing network?
7. How might I use technology to gather people together around my responses?

Livestream: Piper Ramsey

I'm Piper Ramsey. I'm twenty-eight years old, and my handle on TikTok/Twitter/Instagram is @cbfplr.

I'm a child of the internet. I was born in the early 1990s and came to adulthood amidst the era of affordable personal computers, the rise of Facebook, and the birth of the iPhone.

Throughout my life, technology has been my partner as I navigate the world and stay connected to it. The advent of this digital age has radically changed the way we humans relate to one another, and the ability to maneuver those online spaces has become all the more important in the midst of a pandemic.

I currently serve in Northwest Florida. An essential part of what I do is seeking out spaces that the traditional church struggles to reach, and I listen to how the Holy Spirit is already at work. Before COVID-19, this area had a growing number of fresh expressions of church that reached people in pubs, gyms, and on bike trails.

The current crisis proves that adaptability is an essential quality for pioneers at the frontlines of ecclesial experimentation. With the arrival of COVID-19 and the isolation that comes with sheltering in-place, the digital realm quickly became an essential part of how we connect to each other. I find that, through the use of technology, we can create sacred spaces just as fruitful, interactive, and life-giving as any in-person gathering.

Tallahassee Brew Theology is a fresh expression of church that has been growing in the Tallahassee area since 2018. We gather over locally-crafted beers to discuss thought-provoking topics and build a diverse community of "brew theologians." Our community was growing in numbers and beginning to explore discipleship when COVID-19 then prevented us from meeting face-to-face. We have quickly adapted to virtual gatherings and meet more often now than before. Using group chats and video conferencing to join together from our homes, we found the transition from physical to virtual gatherings fairly easy—the Tally "brew theologians" even found a way to continue supporting our local breweries by ordering online!

In the midst of the chaos that came with the COVID-19 pandemic, I found the video-centered social media app, TikTok, to be a place where people found refuge from the isolation and chaos of life-interrupted. The platform has evolved beyond its early days of lip syncing pop songs and outlandish special effects into a complex microcosm of subcultures. TikTok is now a space for quickly-forming communities where comedy and educational creators alike use the app's editing software to convey their messages.

In my role as a public theologian on TikTok, I can post a joke about church culture or a multi-part series on a difficult theological topic—all in one day! The constraints of TikTok's current sixty-second time limit hasn't dissuaded an incredible level of engagement, which is encouraged by an algorithm; in fact, engagement has deepened through easily-made video replies and active comment sections. I'm counted among many pastors, teachers, and therapists finding this silly phone app to be a place where people are loved, the doubters are comforted, and the hungry are fed. It's incredible what God is doing through this social media platform!

The COVID-19 Reset

We all hoped things would go "back to normal" but have found ourselves in a *new* normal.

Both digital natives and digital immigrants alike are familiar with video games. Many have experienced that moment when our system froze up or got stuck in a loop. Whenever that anxiety-inducing moment occurred—whether we grew up on Pong, Super Mario Brothers, or Fortnite—when all else failed . . . we could always hit the reset button!

This is also an approach we employ frequently with the plethora of our digital tools. When our laptop overheats, our PC crashes, or our phone glitches . . . just turn it off and turn it back on. So many times a hard, manual reset seems to fix the issue magically. Many times, our devices become bogged down with cookies, are maxed out with data, or have contracted viruses. The manual reset is a built-in mechanism to optimize and make the system work again.

The church has become bogged down, loaded with unnecessary clutter, and infected with many viruses: the viruses of imperialism, racism, classism, sexism, and so on. The US church has been in a state of plummeting decline for over fifty years. We have needed a reset for a long time.

The global pandemic provided the church with a moment of manual reset.

When the COVID-19 epidemic hit the United States, pastors and church leaders across America were thrust into uncharted territory. Since many state and national leaders called for a stay-at-home order, all non-essential businesses, sporting events, recreational spaces, and large gatherings came to a screeching halt. There was a lot of uncertainty, with many unknowns up in the air for people to ponder, and the church experienced what everyone else had to face: a new normal.

Some states ordered churches to cease services; others, like Roz's state of Ohio, strongly recommended it—meaning it was still somewhat optional. While the governor of Michael's state, Florida, insisted that churches, synagogues, and mosques were "essential" and could keep their doors open if they chose. Fortunately, most churches decided to cease in-person worship regardless.

This caused a tidal wave of people staying at home, leaving many churches scrambling because their buildings were empty and with no physical gatherings taking place.

While larger churches had the opportunity to cultivate an online footprint in the past with the help of financial and staff resources, small to midsize churches with little or no technological expertise experienced a huge learning curve.

No seminar, Bible college, licensing school, or seminary could have prepared pastors, leaders, or staff on how to effectively lead and navigate through the threat of COVID-19. Necessity is the mother of invention, and the pandemic drove the opportunity for innovation and embracing change. Churches seemed to react in two generalized ways, which we describe as responses A and B.

Response A: These leaders saw the crisis as a tremendous opportunity for a reset. They were already facing disruption in demographics and socio-economic decline, so they were asking reframing questions—such as, *What can we do about church, worship, and community?*—before the virus struck. They found in their deepest historical traditions some keys to reimagine themselves in a new world. They learned, prototyped, and created new things. Some began to thrive in new ways they had never imagined were possible.

Response B: These leaders saw the disruption caused by COVID-19 as a monkey wrench in the plan of business as usual. They hunkered down and waited, or they tried to do online what they normally did in person. Others rushed back into physical gatherings, and we saw stories of infection spreading through those worship communities.

The Fresh Expressions movement has always been the canary in the coal mine, alerting congregations to reevaluate what a faith community is, where and when it can happen, and who can lead it. Most congregations seem inaccessible to people not yet in church. A fundamental premise of the movement is that it is only accessible when it emerges from every nook and cranny where life is already happening. This requires simplification, returning to the first principles of scripture and, as we will explore later, recovering a "priesthood of all believers."

This continuous exploration of what "church" constitutes is called, in theological terms, *ecclesiology*, which is from the Greek word *ekklésia*. Originally, the secular term was used to refer to a "political" assembly but in the New Testament, that word accumulates a theological nuance that means something greater than the term *church*. The prefix *ek* (or *ex*) means "out of" or "from." The root word is a form of the verb *kaleo*, which means "to call." Thus *ekklésia* means "those who are the called-out ones."[1] When the church is mentioned, the Greek word *ekklēsia* is used 114 times in the New Testament. For example, see Colossians 1:18: "He is the head of the body, the church, who is the beginning, the one who is firstborn from among the dead so that he might occupy the first place in everything."[2]

When COVID-19 hit our communities, we heard a deluge of sentiments that the church had "shut down" or closed. However, New Testament ecclesiology teaches us that the church is an expression of God's kingdom, which is a liminal place that transcends time and space. And the early church shows us how a movement can grow in an underground fashion with smaller gatherings. Though the early Christians experienced stress from harassment, the stress of a global pandemic led to a scattering of the once-gathered assemblies across the world. Just as Christian faith communities couldn't be closed two thousand years ago and instead acted as a seedbed for a movement, so too can the same outcome be pursued in the present. Many congregations are thriving in the midst of the chaos and disruption.

As a church planter and pastor, I (Roz) continually encourage and remind Mosaic Church of this potential. Here is a letter I wrote to the community during the early part of the pandemic:

Dear Mosaic Family,

I pray that this email finds you safe and healthy. All of you have collectively and individually been in our many prayers.

Just a quick update. Our online worship attendance has been incredible, and you have been engaged in our Sunday worship and opportunities to connect during the week. As a young church, it's remarkable that our finances remain strong due to conscientious, amazing, consistent giving, which is an incredible witness, and our world is in need of this witness from the church right now. We are doing things that we have never done before; our staff is working long and emotionally draining hours, and this support keeps us going and gives us a sense that we are doing the right things. Thank you! In short, COVID-19 has not succeeded in thwarting Mosaic from widening the circle . . . if anything, that circle has grown even wider.

We have been in communication with all our church leaders, and we share with everyone the following information. No current operating procedures for Mosaic will be changing during the month of May. We know that there is an ongoing discussion among state and national leaders regarding the "reopening" of government, economy, etc. The truth of the matter is that Mosaic never closed. We have been fully operational since March 15, albeit in a different and safe format. We have been prayerful and attentive to our state and national political leaders, as well as our local and national health experts. No one "closed" our church, and no one but us will decide when to "open" back up to live worship and other activities at our physical locations.

Our number one core value is safety, and we have felt the weight of that for all of our folks, regular attenders, and staff since the beginning of this crisis. You may have seen the federal guidelines for the recommended "phasing for reopening."

There is precise detail as to what these phases express. Phase one specifically states:

"Avoid groups of more than ten people in circumstances that don't readily allow for appropriate physical distancing."[3]

"Close COMMON AREAS where personnel are likely to congregate and interact or enforce strict social distancing protocol."[4]

"Schools and organized Youth Activities that are currently closed should remain closed."[5]

I have two comments: (1) the guidelines of phase one in no way make corporate worship or children's ministry impossible; and (2) we are in no rush. Worship is happening well with substantial numbers and weekly groups. And online gatherings are taking place and have been well-received. Children's and youth activities are being offered online, and our giving is not currently in crisis.

We feel like we are blessed to wait and that we have a window through which to look out into what emerges as people begin to go "back outdoors." We will be able to observe safely what occurs while continuing with our regular and meaningful all-church ministry. We will evaluate month by month, and we will continue to share with you our formal announcements and decisions, but there is no need to hurry.

Thank you for your stewardship and continued prayers. This is an awesome church and team to have the privilege to lead, even during a crisis. We love and appreciate all of you. Stay safe, and we will continue to keep you advised of further developments.

Grace and Peace,
Pastors Roz[6]

Alongside my wife, as the appointed co-pastor of a 140-year-old historic congregation that is also an incubator of over thirteen fresh expressions of church, I (Michael) am continually reminding our people of the scriptural precedents of the early church and how they have evolved through tradition, reason, and experience. This is the letter Jill and I sent to the WildOnes in the second week of the pandemic:

Dear family,

Our hope was to be back in our sanctuary next Sunday. As we watch this global pandemic unfold in our own country, we are realizing that the effects will be far reaching. We don't know when we will be able to gather physically, but we can safely say it won't be this month.

I know there are mixed emotions about our choice to follow social gathering restrictions. However, let's recall a bit of our Christian history. It is not some brave act of leadership to "have church" in spite of social gathering limits. It's a failure to understand rightly what the church actually is, and it is endangering the lives of vulnerable persons. Christians didn't have dedicated buildings or professional clergy until around 380 CE when Christianity became the official religion of the Roman Empire.

The book of Acts describes what the early church looked like as followers of Jesus met for their gatherings: "Every day, they met together in the temple and ate in their homes. They shared food with gladness and simplicity. They praised God and demonstrated God's goodness to everyone. The Lord added daily to the community those who were being saved" (Acts 2:46-47). By the time the temple was destroyed in 70 CE, they had exited synagogues and were meeting solely in their homes. Under these conditions, for over three hundred years, the church experienced massive growth (millions became Christians across the Roman Empire).

As you all know, the church is not a building that you go to. It is a community of people who derive their lives from the life of God. If we want to be true Jesus-followers, we need to find new ways to plant the seeds of the gospel in the native soils of a digital world, and let it grow wild. This is an act of faith, not of fear.

This is exactly what we are doing with "Living Room Church." Today, over two thousand people joined us for worship. Many visitors experienced our church, and some even gave financially (online) for the first time.

Our team of core leaders has begun to meet weekly by Zoom and is working hard to respond to these emerging realities. First, we need you to respond to the following questions by email or return this insert to the office mail slot:

Do you own a computer, smart phone, tablet, or smart TV? Are you able to operate it to search for things? Are you connected to the internet?

____I have no device and no internet connection.

____I have a device and internet connection, but don't know how to access digital worship.

____ I have a device and internet connection, and I would like someone from the church to help me learn how to access digital worship. Here's my name and contact information_____.

____I have a device and internet connection, and I know how to access worship.

We know there are many children who depend on the school for breakfast and lunch and will be affected by schools' sudden closure. We will now have a drive-through food pantry, practicing proper sanitization and social distancing daily (Mon-Fri) from 12:00 p.m. to 1:00 p.m. at Wildwood UMC. Each child will be provided a lunch for the day and breakfast for the next.

Our core leaders have also organized "Care Bands," which are groups of people to watch over each other in love. If a leader doesn't reach out to you this week, please let Pastor Jill know.

Your health—mind, body, and soul—is our greatest concern.

Sincerely,
Jill and Michael[7]

Recovering a Missional Ecclesiology

As you can see in each of our letters, we were trying to lay out a missional ecclesiology in the simplest way possible. Although our approaches were different and contextually formed, the main ideas are the same.

The nature and mission of the church that we see unfold in the book of Acts can be described as having two primary modes: gathered and scattered. Church assumes a diversity of forms because it is a reflection of the personhood of God, the diverse singularity of the Trinity. The blended ecology of inherited and emerging modes of church life (i.e., form) flow from a God, who is one and three persons (i.e., source).

Jesus, just prior to the Ascension, lays out the missional plan: "Rather you will receive power when the Holy Spirit has come upon you, and you will be my witnesses in Jerusalem, in all Judea and Samaria, and to the end of the earth" (Acts 1:8). We see that spirit power as the churches grow throughout the book of Acts.

We can see an iterative pattern in the earliest portrait of newly birthed communities. As described in Acts 2:46-47, they gathered in the public temple *and* around the dinner tables of their homes. In the primitive church, two distinct kinds of the faith begin to emerge (Hellenist and Jewish; see Acts 6).

"Mission is the mother of theology," meaning we know God because God comes after us. Likewise, the structures of the church emerge as they bend and respond to the emerging missional opportunities. So, we can say that "mission is the mother of ecclesiology" as well. The community forms in our reach toward others, which is a "gathered and scattered" reality, and is consistent throughout the Bible.[8] The movement begins, expanding out from "Jerusalem, Judea, Samaria, and all the ends of the earth." The first wave of backlash forces the disciples to move out from the temple (Acts 8:1), scattering at the edge on the road to Ethiopia (Acts 8:26-27), yet they continue to gather and have a presence in Jerusalem, at their tables. Paul's letters show that even during the subsequent outbreaks of harassment, the Jerusalem church moves underground, but continues to exist there.

On the edge, contextual expressions of the faith begin to emerge. We can see how the blended ecology can work together in a synergistic way in Acts 15. Jerusalem (the gathered church) heard of the tremendous growth among the Gentile converts (the scattered church). However, these two forms of church were as different as the people they were reaching. In the Jerusalem Council, the first attempt to reconcile diversity, they made sharing the gospel of Jesus Christ the main thing. They made major pivots for the Gentiles concerning the circumcision mandate as well as obedience to the 613 Levitical restrictions for devout Jewish Christians (Acts 15:29).

As Paul planted emerging communities throughout the Roman Empire, he encouraged them to nurture good relationships among themselves and the believers in Jerusalem and to collect an offering on Jerusalem's behalf (1 Cor 16:1-4).

This temple-*and*-table form—Jerusalem-*and*-Antioch, gathered-*and*-scattered, collected-*and*-distributed—is an expression of both the stationary and mobile modes of God's presence. Yet, when Constantine legalized

Christianity as the Empire's religion and spread it through conquest, the Jewish and Hellenistic modes largely merged into a single "pull-and-push" model, defined through a standardized form or basic pattern of worship (entrance, proclamation and response, thanksgiving and communion, and sending forth).

Even before COVID-19, we recognized that a pull-and-push model for church (even with attractional features) can't reach most of the population. In times of pandemic, even during harassment and subjugation, the church thrives when it embodies both the attractional features and emerging contextual modes: tabernacle and temple, Jerusalem and Antioch, and collected and sent.

Just as Paul sustained the relationship with the inherited church (while utilizing local synagogues, households, clubs, networks, and so on), so too can every local church utilize the first, second, and third places and shared practices of the larger community. These concepts originate from the work of sociologist Ray Oldenburg. Oldenburg's work defines these as: (1) the first place: the home or primary place of residence; (2) the second place: the workplace or school place; and (3) the third place: the public places (which are separate from the two usual social environments of home and workplace) host regular, voluntary, informal, and neutral spaces of communion and play. Examples of these third places are environments such as cafes, pubs, theaters, parks, and so on.

In a pandemic world, for those of us who are fostering fresh expressions, our two primary mission spaces became closed off; second and third places were going virtual, too, if not fully suspended. We couldn't have Tattoo Parlor Church; the tattoo parlor was closed. We couldn't gather in Moe's Southwest Grill for Burritos and Bibles; they were trying to survive with take-out only. The dog park was empty, as people were quarantined at home, so no Paws of Praise.

This limited us to the only spaces we have left: the first place, or the home. The digital place, or the "space of flows." This led us into recognizing the digital space as its own kind of third place, a missional frontier that many of us had not yet encountered.

31

Ecclesiology is important because people define the meaning of *church* in many ways. Also, our experience of one mode may limit a fuller understanding. Our secular culture has a multitude of opinions, whereas the parishioners who gather in churches have another. For a long time, many have disregarded the need for online worship or for churches even to have an online presence. The argument is usually that the online space can't constitute as a true worship experience or even produce fruit as an evangelistic tool. The old paradigm was to focus simply on the congregation one could physically see, and those who were out could catch some sort of recording or podcast, if that.

Other churches who had an online presence unintentionally treated its viewers as second-class citizens without greeting them. Sometimes they neglected to have any kind of interaction or meaningful engagement because they are unseen in the physical world. So, the online space is something we can accommodate in theory, but doesn't actually count except for boosting attendance if a church counts them in those regards. Even mid-size to large churches have to make the decision between prioritizing the folks in the room or prioritizing its online viewers in terms of setting up the technology, camera angles, and references. It is difficult to do both with limited resources.

The other neglected areas regarding online worship include accompanying wrap-around ministries, such as discipleship groups and classes, membership, or even family ministries. These ideas are often dismissed due to prioritizing the physical environment or participation, and not sensing that online participation could really count or be worth it.

The workforce and secular culture in general understood trends in North America and began to leverage technology a long time ago, as a primary or secondary means of going about their business. Those places were poised and ready for the COVID-19 crisis because they already had virtual workplaces, assistants, and teams working remotely from different cities across America.

And while Americans have embraced busyness with work, recreation, and children's sporting events, Sunday mornings are unfortunately no longer sacred or prioritized to fit into people's schedules. Therefore, an online opportunity could be what they need to meet their needs along with their families' needs. This is one reason why online dating for singles has become a prominent and multi-million-dollar industry, where folks are able to meet people locally in their same cities or even across the country to spark a friendship and potential relationship. In fact, typical churchgoers count themselves as committed while attending a physical gathering once a month.

Another old paradigm for those with an online presence was strictly to view it as the front door of their church. Now, while that has been the case for some, it no longer holds true. The idea was that someone who is interested in your church could potentially visit an online service, and it could convert to their physical presence in a worship gathering. But in many cases that conversion to physical presence never happened and because of that, churches used their online resources as an "in-reach" to those who had at some point come through their physical doors. But what happens if they never attend or have only attended once? As John Wesley said, "The World is My Parish." We predict that Wesley would have been a virtual pioneer in today's society, not as a televangelist but through strategically holding people's attention to accountable discipleship in many different gathering circles.

Attending the physical worship gathering was the only front door effective churches thought about and resourced to reach their communities. Indeed, this is what the church-growth era taught and what Rick Warren made popular with his baseball diamond analogy: the first step for someone to be part of Saddleback Church is to attend worship. Now, that was the case in the past, that if people were going to attend service and keep coming back, then worship had to be at its best. It had to be attractional in nature—we're not putting down attractional worship because it has an important role and place—and seeker-friendly, by making the experience meaningful and offering thoughtful teaching that is easy to grasp. In our time as church planters and pastors, we quickly experienced part of this seismic shift, moving from the attractional model of church and the worship experience to a missional model. We did this by equipping people with the tools and opportunities to make a difference in their world and communities.

Particularly in churches that embrace both worship and discipleship, the sole front door of public worship became food pantries, after-school programs, recovery meetings, ESL programs, community meals, and service days. We began to meet people coming to the churches we served because their encounters were first through some sort of missional arm of the church and not necessarily through a Sunday morning worship experience. The sentiments were predicated on how people wanted meaning in their lives and how they wanted to be engaged in something that was directly making a significant impact. We started to have missional opportunities in the Sunday gatherings. Our missional outreach included: (1) dropping food off at the altar for our food pantry; (2) letter-writing to local schools that had a delayed start to the year because of the nineteen tornadoes that wreaked havoc on Memorial Day in 2020 in Dayton, Ohio, or the frequent hurricanes that devastated Florida in 2020; (3) and even making gift and goodie bags for the local school's sports teams.

We were not expecting the high number of people we met in intentional mission fields that considered us to be their pastors without having ever attended our worship services. We began to realize that even though they are not present in the church's gatherings, they need to matter to us because they matter to God. And in many instances, if the church had a need or was collecting items for a given initiative, they would have been some of the first to write a check or make contact in how they could help. Some church leaders are early adopters with trends regarding "felt need" in the people of their community in an ever-changing society.

COVID-19 catalyzed most churches into a specific lifecycle of innovation. Previously, we had never considered how online worship in this digital age can also deepen and expand the church's reach until we had observed Embrace Church in Sioux Falls, South Dakota. Embrace Church is led by Adam Weber, who planted Embrace with thirty-two people in his first initial worship gathering in 2006. Fast forward fourteen years later, and Embrace has grown to four campuses, with one of those campuses located in Lakeland, Minnesota.

Very early on, Adam made one of his campuses an online campus with the vision of reaching out to its own unique congregation. As Embrace Church's physical gatherings and campuses grew, the online space was no exception. They shared a story over Facebook of a woman who started attending online worship who wanted to be baptized. She flew in from another state for that event because she considered Embrace as her church and Adam as her pastor.[9]

In the first few Sundays of the pandemic, with everyone quarantined and trying to figure out a new normal, there were a record amount of churches streaming online worship, with many churches experimenting with it for the first time. Then it happened. The internet broke. Well, it didn't actually break—but platforms like Facebook, Zoom, and even Life Church's free Online Church Platform couldn't handle the sheer volume of those uploading their services and viewership. The gospel was proclaimed in unprecedented ways that transcended space and even time as people participated after the live airing of worship.

During the first two or three months of quarantine, more churches started to go online, getting the hang of technology with a number of tutorials, trainings, and resources to help in this effort. In the midst of it, churches of all shapes and sizes started to become more creative and innovative by discovering sparks and signs of new life that they were missing or had not experienced in quite a while. Countless churches began to tell stories of how they were reaching people beyond their congregation and started to develop strategies all the way from hospitality, kids and student ministries, discipleship opportunities, and simply fun ways of creating engagement as well as community building.

Churches started reporting large percentages of growth with the attendance beyond the scope of what was once normal for their respective attendance numbers. However, just as there are peaks and valleys in terms of attendance during the year, the same trends are true for online worship. When COVID-19 hit, online attendance and numbers were climbing for the first few weeks, peaking around Easter. But with the oversaturation of accessible content and the fragile state of many folks, those numbers declined in many cases, while in some places still yielding a net gain over previous in-person attendance.

As church planters and pastors, we too witness this with our own churches and so many other churches on what would normally be one of the highest attended Sundays for an in-person worship gathering: Mother's Day. Pastors and church leaders in a variety of settings and Facebook groups were sharing about their frustration around this phenomenon.

We realized that the allure of online worship was wearing off because people were fatigued, distracted, and overstimulated with the amount of content, news, and political issues in our country. Issues surrounding COVID-19, the economy, unemployment, mental health, abuse, addiction, the presidential election, and racism took up people's mental capacity. Thus, many churches had to pivot again by differentiating themselves in the digital space and by meeting the felt needs of those who were struggling by their online presence and pastoral care efforts. It is in these times of uncertainty that people across the spectrum have an openness and a receptivity to receive the gospel for the first time and for others to renew commitments that they had previously walked away from in a past life. God is teaching the church that though buildings have a place and can be leveraged for ministry, those places are only temporary and can disappear in a moment's notice. The denominational and ecclesiastical pressures of fruitful metrics become nuanced and don't matter during a pandemic. God can and will work through whatever medium is available to reach people.

From this point forward, there is no going back to normal. Normal is gone, and normal was not that effective to begin with, if we were to be truly honest. And if we were even more honest with ourselves and our followers, we would admit that most digital worship experiences are ineffective too. COVID-19 exposes churches and leaders to what truly matters in worship and discipleship, in part by leveling the playing field in terms of what is possible in terms of engaging people in a shared Christian life. This experience has also shown us a more expanded understanding of ecclesiology. Through COVID-19, this exposure for churches has also become politized by the parties and branches of government. Through the rush to return to normalized traditions, and reopen for sacred business, we encounter multiple layers of complexity for local churches.

As we are writing now, with vaccines reaching the public, we expect that the normal in-person worship gatherings will happen through several phases. Some of those with regular church attendance in the past will either migrate strictly to an online format or take a hybrid approach. Much of that is attributed to the US Centers for Disease Control and Prevention's (CDC) recommended guidelines, which state that houses of worship are strongly encouraged to follow social distancing measures: remain six feet apart, wear cloth face-coverings, and offer little or no student and children's ministries and nurseries. The concern is to limit exposure to the most vulnerable among us with compromised immune systems, the elderly, and others susceptible to grave illness. We believe this will affect local churches when it comes to attendance. Some won't experience the same attendance numbers as they did pre-COVID-19, some will have to reprioritize budgets and staffing, reimagining their physical spaces, and some local churches will have to close their physical doors.

The immunologists hope we can achieve herd immunity when 60 to 70 percent of the US population is vaccinated. But public gatherings will still face infection risks, much like the seasonal flu, until the virus is eradicated.

Dual Transformation

Thus, we encourage you to be a missionary to your neighborhood as much as to the digital network equally. Every church will need to learn to do this during the pandemic in the digital age. Here's a simple framework to think about how.

Scott Anthony, Clark Gilbert, and Mark Johnson explain that "imminent disruption" is one of the greatest challenges for leaders today. They propose a practical and sustainable process for the transformation of businesses they call "dual transformation."[10] Certainly, for the church we experienced a massive form of disruption with the outbreak of COVID-19. While Anthony, Gilbert, and Johnson apply the concept primarily in the world of business, we have discovered it has massive crossover potential regarding the blended ecology of analog and digital church living together.

Dual refers to two simultaneous transformations that reinforce each other, rather than a monolithic process of change. So, think of two processes of change happening at the same time, like sauce boiling on the stove and bread baking in the oven. Yet we mean *transformation* in its most radical sense: a fundamental change in form or substance. So, the sauce would somehow turn into stew, and the bread would become a potpie. It's not just changing the temperature or the taste, but a complete and total change.

So instead of thinking about transformation as offering what we used to do for in-person worship that moves online, it would be offering a completely new form of worship, appropriate for the digital space.

For the business world, dual transformation involves finding ways to better service existing customers, while simultaneously finding ways to reach new customers outside core markets. And then combining the leveraging of a company's valuable assets for new entrepreneurial ventures.[11]

Dual Transformation

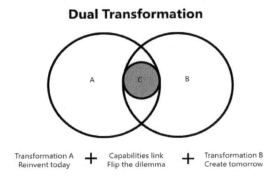

So, there are three key components involved in the process of dual transformation. For a business the components are:

(a) repositioning and improving the business model to maximize resilience;

(b) creating a new growth engine; and

(c) in terms of the "capabilities link," building on the relevant mix of critical assets, brand, and scale, and managing the interface between the core and the new.[12]

For example, Netflix is a company that began with the simple idea that people could rent and return movies through the mail. This eliminated time wandering the aisles of rental stores and cut down on late fees. DVDs were easier to deliver and ship through the mail than VHS tapes, so Netflix partnered with DVD player manufacturers to help drive the adoption of DVDs, which drove the success of Netflix. In 1999, Netflix moved to the monthly subscription model, which allowed unlimited rentals. In 2000, Netflix entertained a conversation about being bought out by their main competitor, Blockbuster, for $50 million. Blockbuster passed on the opportunity and later went bankrupt.[13]

However, Reed Hastings, co-founder of Netflix, always saw DVD by mail as a temporary evolution in the business. He saw the coming potential of downloading and streaming made available by web infrastructure. As the capacity of the internet built up to provide quality streaming, mail subscribers were offered free streaming in 2007. But Netflix launched the streaming-only plan in 2009. This model allowed international expansion in 2010, something that would have been challenging in the mail-only model. Netflix used dual transformation again when it used its streaming business to enter into the film industry, committing not just to deliver the content of others but to create their own. By 2015 the company had transformed from a mail-only service to a web-aggregator service, providing original and third-party content.[14]

Netflix has never stopped sending DVDs in the mail. In 2015, five million subscribers still received DVDs. Each time, Netflix

(a) used and developed existing technologies to provide better service for existing customers (mail-in service),

(b) harnessed emerging technologies to reach new customers (streaming services), and

(c) combined and leveraged their valuable assets to start new ventures (original film and series production).

So, for the church in the digital age, we need to find new ways to care for existing Christians, by doing analog church in fruitful, contextually appropriate ways. Simultaneously, we need to find ways to be a digital church in the flows of a network society. We need to do this while also reaching new people in cyberspace, those whom we couldn't reach otherwise, by forming new Christian communities with them where they are. Combing those modes in new and creative ways forms the hybrid church of the future. This is the twenty-first-century version of a blended ecology of church.

Again, insight from the business world shows that in dual transformation, the greatest challenge lies not in finding creative ways to better service existing customers (or finding fresh ways to reach new customers outside core markets) but in the combining and leveraging a company's valuable assets to simultaneously release entrepreneurial creativity ("Transformation C"). It's the blending together of these two simultaneous transformations in a way that is symbiotic and not parasitic.

The positive dynamics of change must reinforce each other, not replace or destroy the other.

Dual Transformation

Transformation A Strengthen the center Traditioned innovation	**+** Capabilities link Graft the organisms	**+** Transformation B Experiment on the edge Cultivate fxC's
	= Blended Ecology	

So dual transformation requires:

(a) strengthening the center through traditioned innovation, creating and enhancing inherited, attractional, gathered, and analog church;

(b) cultivating missional experiments on the edge, creating and enhancing emerging, missional, scattered, and digital forms of church; and

(c) grafting the organisms together, through connecting, feedbacking, and synergizing.

40

When a local church lives in this dual transformation over time, the blended ecology unleashes new and often unanticipated kingdom flourishing and fruitfulness in the new normal, where we find ourselves. In the next couple of downloads we will show how to do this.

So, what learnings from the quarantine era can churches carry with them to do *analog afresh* in a "new normal?" We will explore this in the next download.

App It

Chat Box

Gather with your team physically or digitally and discuss the following questions.

1. In what ways has COVID-19 been a good reset for your church?
2. What have you learned about yourself during the pandemic, as an individual and with respect to your community?
3. What have you started doing during COVID-19 that you should continue to do indefinitely?
4. What did you stop doing and what should you not do anymore?
5. How have you been "reinventing today" (Transformation A) for how you are being the church?
6. How have you been "creating tomorrow" (Transformation B) for how you are being the church?
7. In what ways can you leverage positive developments to support those changes (e-haviors)?

E-haviors

Consider how these practices might be helpful as missionaries in the digital age.

The Blended Ecology Grid

We believe that for churches to thrive on the new missional frontier, they will need ministries occurring in each quadrant (below).

1. Physical/Attractional: analog, in-person forms of church that employ a "come to us" approach.
2. Attractional/Digital: digital forms of church that employ a "come to us" approach.
3. Physical/Incarnational: analog, in-person forms of church that employ a "we go to them and stay" approach.
4. Digital/Incarnational: analog, in-person forms of church that employ a "we go to them and stay" approach.

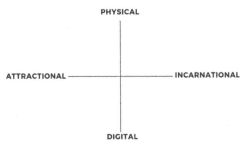

Using the grid above, plot out the major current ministries of your church and where they are on the continuum.

1. Where are your greatest strengths?
2. Where could you do more?
3. How could you get started in one quadrant?

Livestream: Adam Weber

I've been a pastor since I was twenty-four. As of this writing, I'm now thirty-eight years old. I was born and raised in South Dakota, so I really understand this context, at least for people like me who are originally from the area. We have a lot of people with Norwegian and German backgrounds, but we also have a growing population with other backgrounds than that. We encounter a lot of people with Lutheran, Catholic, and Methodist religious backgrounds. I started the church knowing that denominations can be important for people, yet I didn't have the word *Methodist* in our church name because I really tried to be sensitive to those types of traditional differences for people.

Early on, if you required us to say what we existed for, we'd say we existed for young adults, young couples, and the young at heart. We had to really speak into the idea of not just doing things as a checklist to be right with God but to have a relationship with God, which was new to a lot of our people.

For the first few years we struggled to grow, which highlighted the importance of taking our people's social and religious contexts into account. We were a Sunday evening service for the first three years. I knew most people preferred the Sunday morning experience, but I had not yet realized how important it was. Knowing your context *and* listening to your context are critical. In an urban area with a lot of young professionals, time probably wouldn't matter as much, but for this part of the country, maintaining the Sunday morning routine was critical. As soon as we did make the adjustment for in-service times, we more than doubled in size in one Sunday. That's the power of context.

Becoming digital missionaries who use technology to guide people to Christ is a critical aspect of reaching people in 2020 and beyond. For me, avoidance of technology would be similar to going to Mexico and saying, "You have to speak English." That would be unlike Jesus, and it is unkind not to speak the same language that people whom you're trying to reach are speaking. For me, the language is social media. From the start, we were the first church in Sioux Falls to have a Twitter account. We were really the first church in Sioux Falls to engage people on social media, and I did so reluctantly. I wasn't on Facebook when I started the church. My brother was the person who really encouraged me to connect with people on social media. The reluctance to be on social media was what often left the church behind. So, from day one at Embrace, we shared devotional thoughts online.

On Palm Sunday, one of the regional traditions is for churches to have a donkey at the service. So, we decided to take family pictures with a donkey. Then we posted pictures on Facebook and invited people to tag themselves. The next week was Easter, and it brought one of the greatest increases we've experienced in attendance from one Sunday to the next. In two hours, we had twenty-five thousand views on one of the pictures. It was insane!

Now I'm using social media and digital ministry to reach people, but also to help people grow in their walk with God, whether it's an encouraging word or helping with how to read the Bible. YouTube has never been bigger. We're looking at how to use YouTube to reach and grow with our people, which means discipleship. We're considering do-it-yourself videos for basic things our people are yearning and learning to do—from "how to read the Bible" to "how to find someone to date."

We're also entering the podcast channel more intentionally. Our church podcast offers not just our messages but also "Cut for Time," a video podcast featuring content that was cut from the messages. It's something different than what you can get on a Sunday. We offer these on both Facebook Live and iTunes.

Immediately, when COVID-19 hit, we launched eKids online. That's something we've talked about for a long time, but had not yet leaned into. It allows us to create and offer our own content for kids online, and we also use it in-person on Sunday mornings. You can see eKids here: https://iamembrace.com/media/playlist/ekids-at-home-1.

We've continued to critique eKids. Originally, we started with thirty-minute-long episodes and now we're at ten minutes per episode. This means we are trying to listen to what our people are doing and come alongside their limits.

We also launched our "parenting large" group, which is offered in-person and online. We need to continue growing. On our first night, the experience wasn't as strong online as it was in-person, which we don't want to be the case. We want to match the engagement experience as much as we possibly can.

We've talked about holding an online-only service. We've noticed that people don't really like to worship online, so we've talked about offering a shorter service that's more conversational. One of the things I've considered doing is a totally separate service time in the evening with just the message, and keep it really conversational.

It's the willingness to adapt and to make changes to what you've always done.

Hybridity—The Post-Pandemic Church

We propose some key changes congregations should address in a post-pandemic world.

Perhaps the most awesome innovation of the twenty-first century doesn't get enough recognition. It comes from the world of backyard gardening, not Silicon Valley. It's called "ketchup and fries." This is a plant that grows potatoes in the ground and tomatoes up top. Two distinct species are grafted together to form one new living organism. It is an organism from which you can grow both ketchup and French fries. This is a dual transformation organism, and a gamechanger for church potlucks across the country![1]

If you think this is mind-blowing innovation, let us tell you about the Tree of 40 Fruit! This is a single tree that grows forty different types of stone fruit, including peaches, plums, apricots, nectarines, cherries, and almonds. The tree is one of a series of fruit trees created by Syracuse University Professor, Sam Van Aken, using the same grafting technique. Van Aken is an associate professor of sculpture at Syracuse, as well as a contemporary artist who works beyond traditional art, developing projects in communication, botany, and agriculture. The Tree of 40 Fruit blossoms in variegated tones of pink, crimson, and white in spring, then when summer comes the tree bears a variety of diverse fruits.[2]

Reaching back to the image from Revelation 22 that we discussed in Download 1, perhaps a tree "with its twelve kinds of fruit, producing its fruit each month; and the leaves of the tree are for the healing of the nations" (Rev 22:2) sounds familiar? The "tree of life," which we lost access to in the beginning of our story, is made accessible in the end. The tree of life is a "hybrid organism," something once unimaginable to our greatest minds for centuries past. It is deeply significant that we will ultimately do life together for all eternity as a hybrid community grafted together, Jew and Gentile (Rom 11:17-24), around a hybrid organism—a single tree of many fruits.

Hybridity and grafting are from our future, breaking into the present.

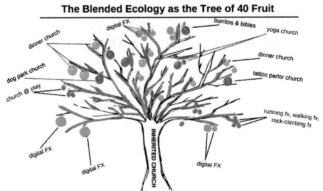

The Blended Ecology as the Tree of 40 Fruit

In some sense, every church that persists in a post-pandemic world is going to evolve as a hybrid organism. We will need to cultivate analog communities that have deep roots in tradition, bioregionalism, and local context. Simultaneously, we will need to cultivate fresh sprouts of church that are nimble and digital, while also having a root-tethered system but appear predominantly in the digital context. Grafting these organisms together could result in a single church that looks like the image above.

Here we suggest some key ideas for a post-pandemic church to thrive in a hybrid way.

Authenticity trumps production value.

The invention of the smartphone and its progression has given everyone the ability and platform to deliver online content. This was a gamechanger, as churches were newly experimenting with Facebook Live and YouTube. They might have had thousands of dollars in equipment with cameras, lights, and smoke machines. Or the audio and lighting might have been lackluster. Every word spoken and lyric sung was not necessarily what you would see from the nation's most visible churches. However, they offered up themselves and their very best to God.

People are looking for something real and someone real they can relate to. It's a well-documented desire for younger generations, but it's also an age-old desire for us all. These churches that were thrust into their digital future overnight had to act fast because inactivity was not an option. They couldn't make a carbon copy of someone else's service, in terms of production value, so they had to be genuine.

A great example of this principle is the famous comedian Jimmy Fallon, of the *Tonight Show*. During the nation's quarantine, people from across America and around the world were tuning into Fallon's nightly weekday segments, *The Tonight Show: At Home Edition*. It gave viewers a day in the life of Fallon, which included taking a tour of his house, meeting his wife and kids, and incorporating them into the segments. Fallon's wife was the camera operator, and his daughters, Winnie (aged six) and Franny (aged five), would play, sing, and interrupt their dad during his monologue and jokes—and simply have fun while he interviewed famous celebrities from their homes through Zoom during quarantine.[3]

Even as famous and glamourous as the *Tonight Show* image had been, Jimmy Fallon was able to capture people's hearts and humor because he related to them and validated a place where everyone was—home.

So, our churches shifted to focus on speaking to what everyone was experiencing. We broadcast worship services from the living room. It created something personal because it was giving people a window into a real worshipper's life and settings. There were no stages, pews, stained-glass windows, or steeples. In many instances it was the person's living room, through an unfiltered lens of reality.

In my case (Michael), with Living Room Church, we moved more fully into a completely distributed form of church. It's a simple concept. Our approach with worship has been not to do the stage production in an empty sanctuary, but to sit face to face with our people and give them an opportunity to be heard and to connect. Each week we have six different living rooms connected on the stream. We've interviewed an "ordinary hero," one of our lay pioneers, who shared how they are processing living through the COVID-19 quarantine.

We pray, sing, sign a digital attendance pad, recite the Apostle's Creed, and take an offering. Our lay preaching team facilitates a sermonic conversation and we then conclude with the Lord's Supper. We worship Jesus separately but together, from our living rooms to your living rooms.

We have no full-time employees, clergy, and no paid technology or production staff. Our volunteer teams learned to run the church with iPhones and laptops, using social media and free streaming technologies. Each person on the team, streaming from their living room, contributed to the worship experiences, while owning the reality of our own quarantine. We shifted from thirty-minute sermon monologues to shorter sermonic conversations, which anyone could speak into through the digital medium. This resonated with people deeply and we began regularly joining new "Network Partners" (a remixed version of membership for people becoming WildOnes from across the country).

Now this isn't the approach of some churches who have the capability of high-end production, which isn't a bad thing—after all, if you got it, use it. However, it's harder to relate to someone on stage preaching to an empty room, reminding you of a place you can't attend. As weeks passed by during quarantine, we witnessed some larger churches and pastors shifting from the stage to their own homes for a more personal experience.

At the end of the day, don't try to be something you aren't, because people can spot a phony a mile away. Be you. Be the church God has called you to be, and be unapologetic about it.

Smaller gatherings will happen more frequently as fresh expressions of worship are created in-person and virtually, in a refashioning of the new normal.

As some people will shy away from in-person mass gatherings, it gives room for creativity in terms of micro-communities. They can meet anywhere, and as people have become reacquainted with their homes, it can reinvigorate home groups and families to form "watch parties" for worship over breakfast. The corporate worship gathering isn't going to disappear, but churches will leverage their facilities to offer smaller and more intimate worship gatherings besides those held on Sunday mornings. It can also be a catalyst for fresh expressions to take place in third spaces, where people are gathering around distinctive affinities, as was the trend pre-COVID-19.

This can be a unique opportunity to empower and provide training for more laity as pioneers leading the movement, as it was in the early Church. COVID-19 changed the way we work, worship, and live. Personally, during the pandemic, we checked in on family members more than ever before. It cost nothing for us to call grandparents over FaceTime with our children multiple times a week, which we didn't do as often before. There is nothing like a pandemic to reflect on what truly matters in our lives.

The use for emerging technology is only going to speed up, intensify, and become more user-friendly. Further, as new generations are born, digital technology will become an ever-more indispensable part of our lives. One of the most popular things people did in 2020 was to Zoom with their friends in order to virtually watch a movie together, share Thanksgiving together, or even have a virtual happy hour. Again, this is just the beginning of a new wave in the digital age. The same thing will happen in terms of worship. People have grown accustomed to worshipping from the comfort of their own home, quite possibly in their pajamas while they drink their morning coffee and move leisurely at their own pace.

Multiple opportunities during the week is the new normal for engagement.

In many phase-one reopening plans for churches, the first step was allowing smaller groups of ten and fewer to utilize a given church's facilities. Parishioners simply reserve a room, practice social distancing, and have their discipleship time together. The usage of buildings will be flipped from open spaces with a large footprint to being more convenient for different groups to gather like never before.

Engagement is more important than attendance and viewership. Many churches began livestreaming their worship services as a starter for their online presence. However, churches of all shapes and sizes experimented to make multiple connections during the week. Mosaic Church (Roz) offered Bible journaling during the week, which is an adult coloring activity on a given topic, and scripture along with a short devotional lesson.

This quickly became one of the most popular offerings, as people were engaging in real time and participating and even weighing in on the conversation. My wife started to participate with our one- and three-year-old daughters as well in the coloring activities, so it became a family affair. Another first for us was to have one of our local musicians, who is a DJ, have a DJ hour over Zoom by playing music requests and creating a time of community. The interesting part was having people join us whom we had never met before. Then we started to offer opportunities for Mosaic kids and students, like online Bible studies, scavenger hunts, and even a birdhouse-decorating contest.

We purchased one hundred birdhouse kits, which we gave away. After everyone picked them up, others who missed out desired a birdhouse. The event quickly went from being "kids only" to including adults. We took time over Zoom to assemble the kits and the following Saturday, contestants showed off the decorated birdhouses to see who would win the best decorated birdhouse. I even heard stories of kids bringing kits to other neighborhood friends who didn't have a home church. The event on the surface was a birdhouse contest, but the real thing that happened was meaningful engagement.

Our family ministries director gave tips to parents on how to disciple their kids during quarantine. All these weekly offerings were followed up with evening vespers by our worship leader, who is a classically trained pianist. Our worship leader would play for about fifteen to twenty minutes when people were winding down in the evening to go to bed. We intentionally decided not to have the pastors as talking heads but instead to incorporate others. And then, once a week, my wife and I offered something we called "Quarantine Conversations: How Not to Kill Each Other During a Pandemic." We talked through communications skills, relationships, inner healing, and forgiveness. Regularly, almost weekly, we had multiple people reach out to us via a private message to request prayer or pastoral care about their marriage and relationships. We also offered other classes, prayer meetings, and discipleship opportunities.

For Wildwood, before the quarantine, we had expanded the life of our church across a seven-day week, making it more accessible to "nones and dones." Almost every day, worshipping communities were gathering in homes, community centers, tattoo parlors, coffee shops, yoga studios, running tracks, Tex-Mex restaurants, and so on. While COVID-19 temporarily shut down many of those places, causing some of our fresh expressions to die, others, such as Digital Yoga Church (practicing yoga together through Facebook Live and YouTube), Supper Table Church (families eating meals together in quarantine connected by screens), and Underground Seminary (a gathering of lay and clergy learning together through Zoom) started thriving like never before.

These technologies literally enable us to be present to some degree across the world at any given moment. A part of us, our digitally-extended mind, is inhabiting both digital and analog space simultaneously. The technology enables an extension of our "self" to be present by bridging the separation of distance. This can be understood as a compression and transformation of time, and the experience of "real virtuality."

We started to offer relationship, and to share in formational Christian practices, connected across space and time through these technological flows. Some of these communities were formed and exist solely in the digital "third place," which is a neutral, communal gathering location for many pre-Christians. Some fresh expressions are hybrids of both digital and analog.

We have learned that the future of the church is not fresh expressions. The future of the church is the blended ecology of fresh expressions and traditional congregations—a manifestation of not only Jerusalem and Antioch, gathered and scattered, tabernacle and temple, but now digital and analog as well. This is being faithful to the deepest ecclesiology revealed in scripture.

We seriously consider how we can be an incarnational presence in this digital space. We are finding that many people we engage with in our digital fresh expressions are bridging back to our Living Room Church (which serves as our "inherited congregation"), and new people in our inherited congregation are pioneering fresh forms of church on the digital frontier.

The temptation post-COVID-19 will present itself as going back to our ministry opportunities in person only. However, we have consciously made the decision not to go back to normal but to surrender into a new normal by offering online engagement.

Prioritize an online service for an online congregation.

The *normal* was for churches simply to stream the services that were happening in the sanctuary. The priority was geared toward the people who were physically present, and the online viewer remained more of an afterthought. However, COVID-19 showed us that the downhome setting of worship was meaningful to people who were also in their homes. Pastors and worship leaders were intentionally speaking on camera to the viewers as the congregation.

The urge is to go back to this type of normal, prioritizing the physical in-person gathering. However, for churches to view the nature of worship beyond their physical sacred space means to experience a separate and stand-alone worship service strictly geared for the online congregation. As we're writing now, the discussion we have had with our own leaders and pastors around the country is to continue this new online campus that was started overnight by necessity. Some will try to return to business as usual, while others will embrace the new normal in this fresh expression of church. It will require more hours, planning, resources, the continued use of technology and a commitment to execute. The fruit may not be visible right away, but consistency, experimentation, and variety will help to create meaningful engagement.

The use of time for an online service for many made it more palatable for personal attention spans. Many churches had to think strategically through worship planning and not cram too much into an online service. In general, at Mosaic Church, like many other churches, we kept it to forty-five to fifty minutes, while an in-person worship gathering would be a length of sixty to seventy minutes.

As preachers, we had a learning curve when moving from preaching a thirty-minute sermon to an in-person congregation, where we could see facial expressions and read the room, to talking into a camera. Many preachers were able to become better at their craft, especially if they cut their sermon in half for online purposes. Preachers had to learn the power of compressing their words in a virtual setting; how to say more with less. Instead of multiple points, outlines, and stories, preachers had to stay on point and because of that, many participants in online congregations were able to retain more content. It also created an opportunity for pastors to preach not only in their homes but also outdoors if the weather permitted it. It allowed for an element of fun, to mix it up, and variety not to get stuck in a rut for multiple weeks using the same format.

Also, worship and discipleship opportunities turned from being a one-sided affair with a leader talking into a camera to then engaging to weigh in with their comments and feedback. On a Sunday it may be difficult for a pastor and staff to greet everyone online, but with certain platforms you can see who joins and welcome people, which creates a personal touch. It is much more than throwing a video on a platform and letting it play. Churches started to embrace real-time engagement with chat hosts on behalf of the church asking questions and responding to the congregation.

Another way we prioritized the online congregation was soliciting multiple folks from our communities on a weekly basis to submit videos leading prayer, reading scripture, and offering a song. We were able to have more people engaged in leading worship than ever before because people had the availability and time to submit a video. Some people were so excited to be a part of worship that they invited family members and friends, many of whom didn't belong to a faith community, to view the online worship experience.

Devote staff time, dollars, and other resources.

Many large churches before the pandemic had an online campus pastor. Meanwhile, many churches who had not previously expanded online will continue their online campuses post-COVID-19 by investing and resourcing it to the next level. They experienced what can be possible, wanting to continue the momentum they developed during the pandemic. We know many churches don't have the resources to hire a fulltime staff member who is ordained and seminary trained. However, there is always a place to start. It may be an unpaid servant leader position for someone who has the skills and talent. Many people would appreciate the opportunity and experience. Wildwood is a good example of a church using teams of unpaid lay leaders and co-vocational ministers. Churches with more financial resources can perhaps offer a stipend or even a part-time position.

The question often posed is this: Must the self-sustaining online congregation be led by a pastor? Each congregation will need to answer that question for itself, based on its needs, context, and polity. For practical purposes, a leader can be an online host who is the "face with the place" to engage people online. A position such as an online campus pastor or host can help oversee online church services, lead a social-media strategy, coordinate details for the weekly stream, manage other unpaid servants associated with the online service, monitor metrics, and create an online engagement strategy to involve people in online discipleship and community life. They can also coordinate watch parties, where small groups host a church service in their homes, which can develop into a fresh expression of a local church. This extensive list might be a lot for one person, but there would be a team developed to spearhead these efforts apart from the current in-person worship service. The opportunities for online worship are numerous, but a post-COVID-19 online campus entails an intentional strategy, planning, and devoted resources.

One other possibility is an autonomous and fresh expression of church with no brick and mortar or physical gatherings that is totally online. As church planters, we represent different schools of thought on the resource capacity needed to seed a church plant as a start-up. It depends on fundraising efforts and outside sponsorships such as denominational support. Some planters will try to "launch large" with a few hundred thousand dollars in start-up funds, while others may have a smaller goal. In the new normal of the digital age, a fresh expression of church that is totally and exclusively digital can begin with a fraction of the cost, depending on the type of technology one chooses. Initially, it takes a smartphone and a computer. One can simply build a fresh-expression gathering from there, with different themes and interests to reach people from the privacy of their own homes. We will share a process for cultivating a digital fresh expression later.

Marry your mission, not your methods.

The old paradigm maintained the message that, "if it isn't broken, don't fix it." For a long time, decline has been the norm in denominations because we became enamored with the methods but did not prioritize the mission. Established congregations get stuck in a rut because they are unwilling to allow change. And the supply of new leaders from seminaries are typically not field-ready because of outdated practices and theological behaviors, which are unprepared for the current reality of making disciples. Jesus said in Mark 2:22, "No one pours new wine into old leather wineskins; otherwise, the wine would burst the wineskins and the wine would be lost and the wineskins destroyed. But new wine is for new wineskins."

Many churches have empty wineskins because change is resisted or neglected. COVID-19 taught at a moment's notice that if you are unwilling to adapt and evolve in methodology, you will cease to exist. By analogy in another enterprise, due to the dominance of big-tech monopolies in most industries, retail store chains were already on the ropes but had to declare bankruptcy with the final economic blows coming from the virus-driven economic downturn.[4]

Some churches that were resistant to change, innovation, and the digital age began to embrace it and surprisingly saw the benefits quickly. However, even during quarantine it is quite easy to get stuck in a rut after early success, which is why churches that continued to see high traffic and engagement continued to nuance their variety and how they delivered the worship experience to their online congregations. In working with our virtual staff, I (Roz) stress that seasons during this pandemic are short. Instead of looking at rhythms in months, we looked at change in terms of weeks, so we don't become too comfortable doing the same thing over and over again. We continue to experiment with our methodology, but marry (commit) to our mission of "being a dynamic mosaic of Jesus-followers."[5]

As a new expression of church, we were used to being portable, agile, and flexible. However, during a pandemic, anxiety and stressors were understandably off the charts, so we did the best we could with the resources we had. After all, the Holy Spirit has a way of infusing it all for the good. In the new normal, the wineskins should be evaluated frequently. The method is typically a vehicle for delivering your church's mission. And the mission is simply the "why?" (For "Methodists," the accountable method of discipleship and the blend of personal and social holiness is inseparable from our mission, but the communication technologies change through the centuries.)

Why do you exist, and what has God called you to do through your unique expression of Christ's body to deliver the message? The willingness to adapt methods to new contexts is brought before God and others in the spirit of humility and transparency.

Move from general to specific.

Throughout the world, the economic hardship during the pandemic continues to be catastrophic. American unemployment rates soared to 14.7 percent and reached over 20 percent for many groups, the highest since the Great Depression.[6] Everyone was scrambling to try to pay their bills, feed their families, and keep their heads above water, all the while waiting for unemployment benefits to kick in. Unfortunately, the system couldn't handle the high volume of requests, which left many Americans waiting for a long time. Along with businesses struggling and some permanently shutting their doors, congregations struggled in an uncomfortable position.

How do we ask people to give during a pandemic recovery where many are facing financial hardship? The paradigm for many churches is a struggle to make the general fund budget, with a small designation to help with benevolence for those in need. However, COVID-19 teaches us that money follows vision and mission. People will give to a cause if they see its direct impact on other's lives, the community, and the world.

Many churches including Mosaic and Wildwood started COVID-19 funds. There were countless stories of providing meals for first responders, helping nursing homes, hospitals, and those that are the most vulnerable in society. At Mosaic Church, we decided to impact directly those in the congregation that were facing dire situations. We met many tangible and physical needs that we would learn about on a daily basis. Our focus shifted from just the general day-to-day financial needs of the church to then providing for those with whom we live, work, and worship.

At Wildwood we shifted to a daily, drive-in food pantry that fed thousands of families. We saw the isolation and trauma and then created digital fresh expressions that created community around supper tables at home and healing through the restorative practice of yoga. We invited people to find relief through artistic expression. We found new ways to be in mission, and the giving followed. The results in some churches were also astounding. We saw an uptick in giving because we were casting a vision and sharing stories of people who were being helped during these trying times.

The new normal, then, will mean for churches who want to remain vital, to continue to focus more of their resources and efforts outwardly instead of merely paying the bills. Of course, as pastors, we understand the need to meet budget and stewardship as a crucial part of our discipleship journey. However, the more that churches can be open-handed with their resources, the more God is given the opportunity to multiply the impact and finances.

App It

Chat Box

Gather with your team physically or digitally and discuss the following questions.

1. Where could you move toward more authenticity and less production value?

2. How could you allocate more volunteer team or staff time to digital church?

3. Where have you been more married to your methods than to your mission?

4. How might you encourage the cultivation of small groups in your church?

5. How might you offer more opportunities to gather throughout the week?

6. What technologies might you use to facilitate these multiple smaller gatherings of people at different times?

E-haviors

Consider how these practices might be helpful as missionaries in the digital age.

1. **Never start your day with a screen:** Many people grab their phone shortly after waking up. Put your Bible by your bedside. Start the day with prayer and scripture reading. Resist the urge to jump right into the digital world.

2. **Schedule your screen time:** To be a digital missionary you will need to be in digital space. But the danger is draining away your time in the shallows. Schedule the times when you will go online each day and have the discipline to stop when your time is up.

3. **Quick updates:** Use social media platforms to post short but frequent updates about your church and life. To make connections in digital space you need to start conversations in digital space.

4. **Show transparency:** Most people post what they think people want to hear. Only post things that are authentic and real. Don't be afraid to be vulnerable but be careful not to bleed all over other netizens either!

5. **Resist retribution when attacked:** As a Christian in the global village of cyberia, people are watching you: how you interact, how you post, what you talk about. When someone curses you, always respond with a blessing. Be intentional to "Love your enemies. Do good to them that hate you. Bless those that curse you. Pray for those who mistreat you" (Luke 6:27-29).

6. **Post to glorify God, not to build self-esteem:** Your self-worth should not come from likes, loves, or wows. In a digital culture where that's what most people are seeking, be a counter-cultural force. This doesn't mean you have to be constantly spouting Christianese (that's also a huge turn-off for "nones" and "dones"). But you can point to the beauty, truth, and goodness in the world. Showcase God's goodness when it's appropriate.

Livestream:
Heather Jallad

I'm Heather Jallad and I serve in a dual role as the lead cultivator of fresh expressions for the North Georgia Annual Conference of The United Methodist Church and as the pastor of community engagement in a local church in an Atlanta suburb. Digital platforms have been crucial in my regional and local roles. My use of digital platforms provides the means to train, coach, and identify new people and places that are leaning into the Fresh Expressions movement.

I've led fresh expressions–related book conversations that have engaged both laity and clergy and have sparked new ideas about what it means to be the church. I have held coaching sessions with pioneers, trained church leadership teams on the core concepts and characteristics of fresh expressions, and hosted virtual coffee and office hours on Zoom, sometimes sharing these on Facebook to broaden the audience. I host a weekly Facebook Live event on a committed Facebook page to share new ideas, upcoming opportunities, and answer questions about the movement. The Zoom to Facebook Live process has afforded me the opportunity to gather pioneers across the region for conversations about the new frontier the church is navigating. We also discuss what might be possible with the added bonus of inviting others into the conversation.

During the prior year in my new context, we listened and prayed about starting a dinner church gathering. While starting and leading a dinner church for three years in another part of the region, I never would have considered launching a drive-thru model of dinner church. However, due to the pandemic, which is causing very real food insecurity and a sense of isolation for many, the Holy Spirit wouldn't leave me alone about starting this way. I used Zoom to train the new dinner church team. This team is made up of people not only from the church I serve but also from another church in the area. The meals are picked up in a drive-thru format and we gather online to eat and to share a Jesus story, conversation, and prayer via Facebook.

As the lead cultivator of The Common Ground Network, a network of fresh expressions in my local church, I have gathered the pioneer leaders online monthly for teaching, coaching, accountability, and prayer.

Recently I began a podcast called *The Common Ground Podcast* in order to share the stories of pioneers in the region and around the country who are loving and serving their neighbors and building communities of faith in some unexpected places. These stories of fearless faith and listening to God are both inspiring and encouraging new experiments in more places. As a part of the Fresh Expressions US training team, I have been able to lead and participate in live webinars and trainings.

Outside of fresh expressions work, I have gathered friends near and far to engage in conversations around systemic racism, what we are learning, and how we might combat this evil in tangible actions and behaviors. The digital space has enhanced and expanded my work in the Fresh Expressions movement. It has also expanded my ability to form meaningful and impactful relationships and partnerships with a diversity of pioneers and practitioners—connections that would otherwise have proven challenging or even impossible to make.

Digital Worship— Liturgy, Lectionary, and Utilizing Free-Tech

The Greek word λειτουργία (*leitourgia*) means "public service," so for the church we understand liturgy as the "work of the people." However, modern church worship is often not the work *of* the people. Rather, leaders with graduate education work *for* the people. Specialized theological education on university campuses amid the socio-economic rise of college-educated professionals in business, medicine, and science encouraged laity (the people) to take a back seat in the pews. The paid religious professionals naturally took authority in the life of the church.

Many churches have become pastor or staff driven, so much so that lay folks are either not encouraged to participate, or they view pastors and staff simply as their employees. The congregation loses the healthy balance of incorporating laity through liturgy and living into the shared "work of the people."

Many churches neglect the "priesthood of all believers," a phrase drawn from the New Testament sermon to the Hebrews. Ordination is one way to set apart those who are called to vocational ministry. However lay people, then, need to be unleashed in the power of the Holy Spirit to live out their calling, both in the marketplace and in the life of the congregation. This problem is as old as the early church: God calls forth pioneers who are not ordained, not seminary-trained, or without professional degrees but do have a burning passion to see people encounter Christ's love.

We are firmly convinced that the most effective ministry comes from lay people. Clergy and staff need to pour gasoline on their burning bush instead of squelching it. To get a new ministry approved by a board or a committee has been the trap for far too long. The process can be long, or there may be a lack of understanding as to why a ministry or a person needs to be encouraged to take up their calling. Discouragement sets in to strip the church of yet another opportunity. The church has had more potential ministries lost to "opportunity cost" than anything else.

You can see the divide between people and leadership anytime you walk into a place of worship. No matter how historic or modern, you tend to see the stage or pulpit elevated and by design the people are far away from those leading the service. This physical representation for the sake of sight lines and sound has cemented the mentality of separation and misunderstanding. Only a handful of people may be involved in any given service and lay voices, gifts, talents, or abilities tend to go missing. While this may be a reality for many churches, it doesn't mean that it has to be the default future. With advances in technology and the unfortunate circumstances around COVID-19, numerous congregations have cultivated fresh expressions or have found new ways of reaching people through many different platforms, featuring the involvement of lay people to carry out the work.

Many churches who were on the fence about how to use technology pre-COVID-19 have now found novel ways of connecting with people in meaningful ways. What we share is not a "how to," but a general description of what they have witnessed, experienced, and practiced on this journey. Perhaps you can find the models and methods that work for you and your context.

Crowdsourcing and Engagement in Worship

Depending on whether you livestream, pre-record, or use a different digital platform, there is technology useful for incorporating many voices in a worship experience. The technology doesn't need to be fancy or cost thousands of dollars. It can be done on a shoestring budget. Engagement is the name of the game, and this means *having a conversation.* It means treating people at home not as observers or spectators but rather as participants in the worship experience.

Video Testimonies

One easy and effective way for involving a variety of voices in the church experience is through video testimonies. Public speaking is one of the most common phobias people have, so there are some folks who may not have the courage to speak in front of a live audience. However, for some, speaking into a smartphone or camera feels more like having a casual conversation. They are not staring out into a sea of faces or from a podium where they feel disconnected and elevated from the congregation.

A simple *at home* atmosphere can make a video testimony feel comfortable for an online audience, as if one were "pulling up a chair" in someone else's home. We mentioned in Download 2 that during the CO-VID-19 quarantine, many celebrities produced their shows from home. For the most part, those episodes were unscripted and generally fun, as is expected of Fallon. He was not dressed up in his TV-ready suits but was as casual as one can be, donning a T-shirt and jeans. Even after returning to *The Tonight Show* after quarantine, Fallon is still looking more casual in his clothing, which makes him more relatable to the viewer at home.

Video testimonies can create a similar feeling because we get a glimpse into some else's daily life. Share with the congregation or your network as to the "why" before you introduce the "how." Cast a vision for how a video testimony is important in the life of the congregation. It need not be complicated, but testimonies are essentially short stories detailing something God has done in a person's life. They are an essential part of evangelism, even on screen.

A testimony encourages a church body and helps to increase faith. People may not always relate to the pastor or paid staff, but when a lay person shares their testimony there is likely someone listening and going through a similar set of challenges. Before casting the net, set the vision in place. Once the vision is set, give people some easy handholds so they can share what comes easily and simply to them. An easy format for testimony can be shared under the heading, "What do I say?"

- Introduce yourself.
- Your past: Tell us who you were before you met Jesus.
- Your encounter: Tell us when you met Jesus and what the encounter was like.
- Your transformation: Tell us how your life has changed.
- If other people are involved in your story, please don't include their names.

Keep these testimonies concise. Many of us are aware that the saturation of information and entertainment has reduced a person's attention span. A testimony shouldn't be lengthy and should preferably be completed in five to seven minutes. Provide directional guidelines to those sharing their testimonies or preparing any video segments for worship. This will help them feel at ease. Explain how to share the image file with the media director, team, or unpaid servant responsible for piecing the elements together. A few small details about process can prevent a person from agreeing to do it if they are not able to capture a video with their phone and share it with someone else.

Best Practices for Filming

- Use the horizontal orientation on your smartphone device.
- Use a stable surface or a tripod to place your phone on and don't simply hold the phone with your hand.
- Use three seconds of stillness or silence before and after shooting your video.
- Record in a quiet area and avoid background noise, especially the wind if outdoors.

- Use natural light whenever possible.

- Keep a three- to five-foot distance between you and the camera.

- Look directly into the camera and avoid looking down or off to the side.

How to send the file? This can be a challenge for those who are not technologically inclined, but it is definitely something that can be overcome with the following suggestions:

- Google Drive: You can create a free Gmail.com account, upload a file to it, and simply share it.

- Onedrive: Most people who use Microsoft Office work from Onedrive and can share a link to media files over email.

- WeTransfer: This is a free web resource, and no registration is required. As long as the file is under two gigabytes (2GB), it can be set to the intended audience. You can access WeTransfer here: https://wetransfer.com/.

- Zipped File: If the file is only slightly too big for email, you can "zip" it to make it smaller and attach the zipped file instead. (However, most businesses where people work will not permit a zip file past their firewall due to potential hidden viruses.) The recipient receives it, and then can "unzip" it and have your original video file. Then attach the zip file to an email and send.

- Vimeo: If you have a Vimeo channel, upload it to your Vimeo account and say that anyone can view and download it, but put a password on the video so that it won't really be public.

- DropBox or Box: You can upload the file to DropBox or Box and share it with your intended recipient (make sure your preferences are set to allow downloads without having an account).

Video testimonies don't have to be presented every week; rather find a rhythm for your own context and incorporate diverse individuals who represent your congregation. However, since technology transcends geographical space and time zones, there can be ample opportunities to have guest preachers and even powerful testimonies from anywhere around the world. The key is asking individuals and getting their written permission and consent to use any particular video that could help in your worship experience.

Music

Worship through song can be reimagined in an online environment, and the style of music can be different from what you presented in person. Again, depending on your context and congregational make-up, it could be an opportunity to include a diverse representation of musicians and singers. The key is variation, and not falling into a monotonous state with music. Much like testimonies, you can recruit guest musicians from all around the world too. It doesn't have to look the same every week, and it could also be either recorded or live from a person's house, church facility, a third space, or even outdoors.

One of the major learning curves for congregations and fresh expressions is that the length for an online music format should be shorter than an in-person format. Since the COVID-19 pandemic began, you may have heard the phrase, "I am Zoomed out." Our attention span is shorter, we find ourselves staring at a screen now more than ever, and most won't give their full and undivided attention to a video streaming service that is sixty to seventy-five minutes long.

In many online communities the maximum for engagement is forty-five minutes and under. It may seem short; however, it focuses worship leaders on the essentials. Instead of a twenty-five- to thirty-minute sermon, compress it to fewer than twenty minutes. Instead of doing three to four songs, consider singing and presenting a total of two songs.

More variation is needed to maintain engagement when a worshipper can walk away without being seen. There can be a mix of musical styles: contemporary, classic or traditional, gospel, blue grass—the sky's the limit. The key is for it to be worshipful and done well. Your usual worship leader can recruit outside their own immediate network or give other emerging leaders an opportunity.

Moderate the variation through a mix of music that is familiar and new. Lyrics on screen can encourage an online congregation to sing along from home. If a song is newer, and there are no lyrics provided, it becomes a performance rather than a worshipful moment for the participant. As soon as people become observers in online worship, they are likely to tune it out altogether. Engagement is the name of the game, in both the digital age and during in-person gatherings.

Readings

The ability to reimagine worship in the digital age can come from a simple act of scripture reading. The scriptural text from a sermon can easily be read by different people within a congregation or community. It's not hard to pull off and some people will be honored that you asked them. A few may reluctantly accept, and fewer may say no altogether because they don't want to watch themselves online.

Can you imagine what it would look like to engage at least over half your congregation as active scripture readers in worship? When people within a community see someone they know in an online worship celebration, it creates synergy and buy-in from others. It can tear down the divide between laity, pastors, and church staff.

To incorporate yet even more people, have a daily or weekly online scripture reading. It can be the verse of the day or week that many people can rotate throughout the congregation. It doesn't have to be fancy; nor does it need to be a devotional, homily, or sermon. It's simply sharing the scripture verse for people to meditate on throughout the day or week. This is the reason so many online, new-age spirituality applications are successful today. They provide users with the affirmations they need, all of which can be shared and accessed at any time. Also, the environments like many of the other segments can vary and take place from wherever will be familiar, interesting, and fun.

For those who use the lectionary, ask what it would look like to incorporate several others on a worship team in planning for an online presence. The digital age is not reserved for alternative or contemporary settings. It can be used effectively online with engagement through familiar, traditional music; scripture reading; guided meditation; and testimony that features the work of a faithful people. You can incorporate more individuals, groups, and families to share from the Old Testament, the Psalms, and the New Testament.

Family Moments

Online worshipping communities and fresh expressions are typically geared toward adults. However, one of the most challenging segments for fresh expressions would be families with children. Roz, with three kids aged three and under, knows how hard it may be to participate in an online service. When adults are the focus, it can come at the cost of losing families or alienating them from the corporate worship experience. Church sanctuaries have dealt with this problem since the beginning, and many have resorted to special programming for young children during adult worship. Since engagement is not restricted in the digital space to one hour live at 10:30 a.m., ten minutes of pre-recorded special worship programming for young children might be an alternative.

COVID-19 closed school buildings and rushed our children into remote learning. Kids are in front of a screen for several hours each day, having to focus and sit still, expected to keep up like they would in a live and interactive classroom setting. It is unrealistic for kids or even older students to sit for an online worship experience unless there is something for them be engaged with. So, this challenge is a great opportunity to incorporate families into the life of the online church body. It can freshen up anything that has gotten stale or routine from week to week.

A children's moment during worship geared toward families and kids can be led by a children's minister or lay person. In many congregations the children's moment can be the most engaging segment during in-person worship. Teaching children the importance of worshipping together is arguably the most important thing of all, as they carry this conceptual framework with them into adulthood. Online, it can create a special moment for kids to have a moment of fun and learning. It can also be something for the entire family when parents and grandparents are challenged by family devotions and spiritual growth. The children's segments can be broadcasted weekly or in whatever timeframe that suits your context and capacity.

In addition to a children's moment, consider a kids and student "take-over" of the online worship celebration. The service can be mostly organized by kids, students, and families with the help of the pastor or worship leader. These occasional special services can serve as a catalyst for variety, incorporate diverse voices, and allow people to use their gifts, talents, and abilities. It also empowers younger generations to recognize and use their gifts. Families can get excited about it and invite other family members who may not attend or regularly view the worship celebration to do so in a fun, inviting format.

In addition to kid and student Bible studies, there are other ways to build interaction and engagement. Creative activities include scavenger hunts, show-and-tell for preschoolers, and other interactive games. Prioritizing families in a digital age is urgent if we intend to reach new generations through discipleship efforts.

Monologue to Dialogue

Download 8 is fully devoted to this idea, so here we anticipate a couple key ideas. In the past, the sermon and worship experience became more of a one-sided monologue, contributing to the disconnect between the pulpit and the pews. The monologue is how preachers developed the art of preaching for centuries. However, in a post-Christian world, a twenty-five-minute monologue often doesn't connect, especially with an online audience.

In this post-modern, digital age, worship and the sermon can become more of a multi-direction dialogue.[1] Westwinds Church did something interesting with Twitter before the pandemic. A reflection question is asked by the host, pastor, or worship leader when the service starts. The congregation (now online) is then asked to submit a particular answer, thought, or question during worship. However, it doesn't stop there, but the pastor or host is then able to respond live to the individual, not only in the web-conferencing chat but also by addressing him or her during the sermon or toward the end of it. Interaction and engagement are a great help in forming a connection with online worshippers.[2]

Another segment connected to the sermon is having a talk-back seminar session following the sermon. It can be done immediately after worship or later that evening. The key is diving deeper into what the scripture or message teaches, the ability to ask questions and give reflections. A dialogue can occur between the host or pastor and congregation, and also within the congregation.

Crowdsourcing

Crowdsourcing (capturing input via a video request) is trendy for churches that desire to hear from the congregation. It can be included throughout an online worship celebration or as an intro loop. It can be as simple as how are you *really* doing right now? Or what do you love about ___church? What are you looking forward to in this new year? Or it can even be targeted to a specific season and the feelings that accompany it. Whatever it is, it fosters engagement and incorporates a variety of voices in worship. The videos can either be all pieced together, or a few can be shown every week in a given series. But first, I offer a word of caution: do this occasionally and not over-ask because it can wear out your congregation or community. One idea is perhaps to do it sporadically over the year and drive home whatever vision or message you would like people to walk away with.

Many other segments can be created for an online worshipping community, and fresh expressions that can incorporate all of the given body instead of solely the clergy, religious paid professionals, or church staff. This current digital age can be used as a vital tool to level the playing field and give laity the opportunity to participate in the virtual liturgy where it can truly be the *work of the people*. To demonstrate, we invite Tesia Mallory, a master of creating digital worship using liturgy and lectionary, to share in the livestream below!

App It

Chat Box

Gather with your team physically or digitally and discuss the following questions.

1. What suggestions in this download seem most useful for your context?

2. Name some creative ways you have used crowdsourcing?

3. How have you made space for testimony sharing in your setting?

4. Is your worship accessible to families? Why or why not?

5. How might you more effectively involve more people in the work of worship?

6. Is your tendency to stick with the same formats and rhythms, or do you switch it up?

E-haviors

Consider how these practices might be helpful as missionaries in the digital age.

1. **Before you share, fact check**: A massive amount of misinformation saturates the internet. Try to avoid sharing things that are false. Do some research to determine whether something can be validated.

2. **You vote with your clicks**: In the attention economy, what you pay attention to and engage with is being monetized. Algorithms in the social media system are designed to get you to consume. If you fall for clickbait, you enforce the system. Never click an advertisement! The algorithm will not let you easily forget it.

3. **Follow people you disagree with**: Social media also creates silos and echo chambers. The algorithms work to connect people with similar perspectives. Be intentional to engage with people who think differently than you do.

4. **Use the "unfriend" or "unfollow" features sparingly:** In the digital world, as they say, "easy come, easy go." People quickly sever relationships with people after disagreements. This creates a superficial level of relationship. We personally make a commitment never to unfriend or unfollow anyone we relate to. Jesus doesn't turn his back on us when we act crazy, and we shouldn't do it to others. Of course, situations of abuse or stalking are an exception to the rule.

5. **Love on people:** Be a cheerleader for others. Don't always post about yourself. In your pre-planned time on social media, pray for God to nudge you toward people that need a word of hope or encouragement. Randomly remind someone how awesome they are.

6. **The invite cascade:** Your posts, events, pages, and groups can expand beyond your personal circle. Encourage people involved with what you're doing to start "invite cascades." This has great missional potential to reach people outside your own social media network.

Livestream:
Tesia Mallory

My name is Tesia, and I'm the director of worship at United Theological Seminary, as well as at Stillwater Church in Dayton, Ohio.

I have my own culture consulting and coaching business—and I work with local churches, pastors, and worship leaders as well as the West Ohio Conference of The United Methodist Church. It's my passion to equip local churches and worship ministries.

Considering worship online, thinking of the lectionary and the church year—they all fit together very well. So the lectionary is a kind of scripture guide of lessons that the "big C church" has given us, and it's been used for most of church history. The lectionary church year is a rhythm that Christians can orient themselves with, and it's counter to the cultural rhythm.

For example, there's a Christian new year, which is the first Sunday of advent, and then there's the cultural new year, which is January 1—but they orient us in a different way. We can dig even deeper into the church year and into the lectionary with the need for more rhythm in our lives. This is truly tapping into the tools that the church has given us. The lectionary can help us orient our lives around who Jesus is in a deeper way.

So, when I think of small groups, for example, the lectionary gives you scriptures for every day of the week. You could have small group leaders conduct Bible studies around them or practices where you just listen to the scripture being read and ask simple questions like, What did you hear? How is God speaking to you through this? That's a practice called Lectio Divina (you can Google that!). You can search for lectionary texts at https://www.umcdiscipleship.org/calendar/lectionary, and it will give you daily readings.

You can do this with kids too. There are a ton of resources out there for scripture lessons. You can ask them what's going on in the story? Just reading the Bible stories helps them learn and connect. Scripture can be read in your house, and you can digest and talk about it as a family or community. It's a great way to connect with God in a different kind of ancient way.

Breathing exercises are also becoming mainstream. They're an effective way to alleviate anxiety in the body. There are a ton of other practices too. There are prayer beads (good for crafty people), where you thread beads onto a string and wear them as a necklace—and then hold the bead while you say a prayer, with each bead signifying something different. You might pray for the world, your community, your family. You pray for those who need healing. And it's a way to use your hands physically to join your hearts in prayer. And kids can get crafty with those things. Another thing going back to *Lectio Divina* is, instead of just saying you're reading the scripture, ask what is God saying to you through it? Instead of typing it out, you can also paint or do other artistic things with it. All this helps in planning and designing digital and analog worship.

Digital Incarnation— Rethinking Evangelism and Discipleship

I have a lot to tell you. I don't want to use paper and ink, but I hope to visit you and talk with you face-to-face, so that our joy can be complete" (2 John 12).

John expresses two things: (1) I have a lot to say, but not through a mail courier; and (2) we've stayed connected through these letters but being "face-to-face" will make "our joy complete." I'm using this technology, but long to be with you in-person.

Paul's letters have a similar sentiment. The Apostle is using the technology of written letters to communicate to communities of faith, with individuals who had personal relationships with him. In a purely practical evaluation, we can see that Paul was using writing technology

- to encourage, correct, and guide churches he himself played a role in planting;

- to encourage, correct, and guide churches he had not yet met with in-person;

- to encourage, correct, and guide churches he was disconnected from physically due to travel or imprisonment; and

- to sustain personal relationships with fellow missionaries and his protégé.

The apostles used the written word delivered through the flows of the *cursus publicus* (Latin for "the public way"), which was the courier and transportation service of the Roman Empire. The first disciples used a complex web of older and emerging technologies: oral tradition, written word, road systems, and mail courier.

Christians have always adapted the emerging technologies for the expansion of the faith. Paul's uses of these technologies helped the first scattered churches communicate and multiply. Early Christian adoption of the codex preserved and spread the Gospels. Johannes Guttenberg's printing press fueled the Reformation. Billy Graham's use of stadiums, microphones, and speakers in his evangelism crusades, gave birth to the first modern megachurches.

We mentioned earlier how the traditional church utilizes multiple layers of technology that would have been considered strange or even idolatrous to generations past (electricity, projectors, microphones, PowerPoint slides, etc.). It is hypocritical to judge emerging technology while gripping tightly to our own. Critically evaluating the technology of a new generation, as well as the technology of our own inheritance, is important.

Like the great cloud of witnesses before us, we have utilized technology to sustain our churches throughout the pandemic. We have discovered how to reach people across the United States whom we would have never reached before. Even as vaccines for the pandemic are made available, many of us will continue to connect in this way.

But like John and Paul, we can say that we long to see you "face-to-face" so our "joy can be complete." As we have advocated throughout this book, we believe a "both/and" approach of analog and digital is the key to missional vitality in the digital age.

Does Digital Bring Us "Back to the Future"?

In some ways going forward into digital is bringing us back to the oral culture in which the early church was formed. In *Oral Tradition and the Internet: Pathways of the Mind,* the late John Miles Foley, an American professor of folklore and oral tradition, demonstrates that our oldest and newest technologies of communication are in many ways fundamentally equivalent. His book illustrates and explains the deep similarities and correspondences between oral tradition and the internet. In contrast to the fixed, linear, line-by-line spatial organization of the printed page, the technologies of oral tradition and the internet mirror the way we humans think by processing along a network of pathways within a network.[1]

Anthropologists Martindale, Shneiderman, and Turin studied indigenous communities with rich storytelling cultures and oral traditions. Martindale et al. studied how these indigenous peoples engaged textual and, later, digital technologies. From their work with the Thangmi people of Nepal and northeastern India and the Tsimshian people of the North American Northwest Coast, they discovered important aspects of "communal memory." They write, "Memory is not a singular enterprise; it emerges as conscious recollection from embodied knowledge or experience, a process that often, for these Indigenous societies, links orality and performance in a powerful dynamic."[2]

Consider how textual literature limits communication to an exchange between an author and a reader. Oral and digital platforms "promote iterative and lateral connections in which information is transmitted quickly within and between groups, mimicking the practise of collective rituals. In this way, Internet technologies and oral traditions share a core dynamic, enabling disparate individuals to navigate rich social networks to create patterns of meaning."[3]

Oral tradition, or oral lore, is an ancient kind of technology. It is a form of human communication wherein knowledge, art, ideas, and cultural material are received, preserved, and transmitted orally from one generation to the next. The transmission occurs through speech or song and may include poetry, folktales, ballads, chants, prose, or verses. Oral tradition enables a society to "transmit oral history, oral literature, oral law and other knowledge across generations without a writing system, or in parallel to a writing system."[4]

Traditional oral cultures formalize and solidify memory over generations. In a world of textual documents, this may seem foreign to us. But ancient and current peoples, such as the Tsimshian and the Thangmi, have built an intellectual edifice of orally transmitted narratives that recount the detailed history of their families since the Pleistocene era. As Martindale et al. explain, "Although Western scholars and courts of law have questioned how stories told only as oral narratives can possibly be historically accurate, recent archaeological work has shown that Tsimshian narratives correctly recount millennia of history."[5]

Oral transmission moved into letter writing in many human societies, which relied on increasingly sophisticated recording techniques—ochre and rock, paper and pen, keyboard and screen—to document the world around them and assist them in the mission of recall. Yet both oral and digital technologies foster "co-creative, participatory, and ever-emergent experiences in which deeply embedded memories and new experiences are brought together to create cultural coherence."[6]

Hebrew tribes carried the stories of their faith through oral tradition for centuries before they were written down. Many then memorized the entirety of the scriptures. For example, at the time of bar mitzvah (age thirteen) Jewish males memorized the Torah (Pentateuch), the *Nevi'im* (the Prophets), and the Kituvin (the Writings), which comprised all of the Hebrew scripture, Tanach. Early Christians were deeply formed in the culture of oral transmission and utilized the technology of the written word. The Gospels were most likely carried on orally for a period of time before they were written down. Christianity became increasingly a religion of the written word when that technology was becoming widely available across the Roman Empire.

The success of the Protestant Reformation has been widely linked to the invention of the printing press by Johannes Gutenberg. The use of this technology to reproduce Bibles made the sacred texts accessible to the everyday literate people. This unleashed a new iteration of a "priesthood of all believers."

McLuhan writes, "With Gutenberg, Europe enters the technological phase of progress, when change itself becomes the archetypal norm of social life." He goes onto say, "Print, in turning the vernaculars into mass media, or closed systems, created the uniform, centralizing forces of modern nationalism."[7] It is hard for us to approximate the impact this technology has had on humanity. It has not only rewired our brains and how we process information but also restructured the structure of human society.

What McLuhan called the "Gutenberg galaxy" enjoyed a long life, spanning well into the modern area. He states that while it was theoretically dissolved in 1905 with the discovery of curved space, "in practice it had been invaded by the telegraph two generations before that." Emerging discoveries in physics disrupted the linear line-by-line Newtonian logic that reigned for generations. But it was this technology that allowed bits of data to travel at the speed of light that would finally disrupt this dominant technological paradigm.

While most Christians may be slow to engage with the emerging technologies of the digital age, other groups have not been so reluctant.

Where Are the Healers?

"Where are the healers?" This question emerged in the middle of the pandemic, as thousands of people were dying every day and morgues were running out of refrigeration spaces to store the bodies of fallen loved ones. We were forced to ask questions, such as: "How did Christians respond to previous pandemics?", "Where is the church's response to this crisis now?" "Where is our power to heal?", and "What message does it send to the world when we are no longer first-responders but can even be non-responders (or worse, be in denial)?"

During the onset of the COVID-19 outbreak, Len Sweet streamed a reflection using Facebook Live, in which he playfully reflected on the fact that most seminaries offer courses on pastoral care, preaching, and church management, but with few exceptions no courses on healing.[8] Isn't that a central call of the church? If so, why neglect training Christian leaders in how to be healers?

We inhabit, reflect on, and teach about Luke 10:1-9. We consider this to be Jesus's missional blueprint for a pre- or post-Christian world. It reads:

After these things, the Lord commissioned seventy-two others and sent them on ahead in pairs to every city and place he was about to go. He said to them, "The harvest is bigger than you can imagine, but there are few workers. Therefore, plead with the Lord of the harvest to send out workers for his harvest. Go! Be warned, though, that I'm sending you out as lambs among wolves. Carry no wallet, no bag, and no sandals. Don't even greet anyone along the way. Whenever you enter a house, first say, 'May peace be on this house.' If anyone there shares God's peace, then your peace will rest on that person. If not, your blessing will return to you. Remain in this house, eating and drinking whatever they set before you, for workers deserve their pay. Don't move from house to house. Whenever you enter a city and its people welcome you, eat what they set before you. Heal the sick who are there, and say to them, 'God's kingdom has come upon you.'"

This passage lays out what we call the loving first cycle proposed for cultivating digital fresh expressions. But we start with perhaps the most neglected aspect of the text, "heal the sick who are there" (Luke 10:9). Luke connects entering a space, eating at tables, and curing the sick who are there, all in a single missional movement.

Break it down like this:

- Enter
- Eat
- Heal
- Proclaim

We often emphasize the incarnational nature of entering the world of our "other" in a posture of vulnerability. Of course, we get excited about the eating part, after all, here is theological validation for the potluck! The preachers among us get very excited about the proclamation piece. But what about the healers? Where are they?

Churches make the front page a lot these days. Especially during the first stages of the COVID-19 outbreak, when we saw the unfortunate stories of churches being "super spreader events" of the virus, in which many lost their lives. When's the last time a church was on the front page for healing the sick?

Jesus of Nazareth healed the sick during his earthly ministry (Matt 9; Mark 5:25; Luke 5:12; John 5:2). Christian pioneers who took Jesus's call to be healers created the first medical systems. While ancient Rome had military hospitals, St. Basil of Caesarea founded the first hospital to care for the poor and sick in 369. Christian hospitals spreading across both the East and the West so rapidly that by the mid-1500s there were thirty-seven thousand Benedictine monasteries alone that cared for the sick. Albert Jonsen writes,

> The very conception of medicine, as well as its practice, was deeply touched by the doctrine and discipline of the Church. This theological and ecclesiastical influence manifestly shaped the ethics of medicine, but it even indirectly affected its science since, as its missionaries evangelized the peoples of Western and Northern Europe, the Church found itself in a constant battle against the use of magic and superstition in the work of healing. It championed rational medicine, along with prayer, to counter superstition.[9]

One of our core identities as the church is to be healers in a COVID-19 world. Steve Hollinghurst notes that one of the most disturbing aspects of recent surveys around suffering, spirituality, and the church, is that none of the respondents understood how these things were even connected. The church simply had no relevance to the big questions of life, suffering, and sickness. It was not understood to be addressing society's ills in any meaningful way.[10] Further, amid COVID-19 we have largely failed to claim a moment of reset.

However, there have been many stories about the "healers" in our society. They are the frontline care workers. Overnight, these people, who usually played a role in society that is often overlooked, became our heroes. Nursing is often a tough and thankless job. Yet these nurses soon came into public awareness in a new way.

Who didn't cry when we saw the medical workers praying together in New York City? Who wasn't moved when people lined the streets in cities all over the world to applaud and praise the hospital workers as they walked home exhausted from their shifts? We experienced our generation's own version of a war, a pandemic equivalent to the Spanish Flu of 1918, or the Bubonic plague of the mid-1300's. We rallied together to demand appropriate Personal Protective Equipment (PPE) for these modern-day healers.

Alicia Keys provided the ballad for our age, live on CNN's *Global Town Hall*. The song "Good Job" showed images of nurses, doctors, janitors, and cashiers, risking their lives to work on the front lines of the pandemic.[11] In a sense, Keys sang humanity back to God with a hymn to the sacredness of work. She showed that a true "priesthood of all believers" sees every job as a holy act of co-creation as a "good job." She exposed the false dichotomy between the sacred and the secular that damages the very relational fabric of society. The divide is what Jesus already healed long ago on a cross.

As Martin Luther once said, "Every occupation has its own honor before God. Ordinary work is a divine vocation or calling. In our daily work no matter how important or mundane we serve God by serving the neighbor and we also participate in God's on-going providence for the human race."[12] For just a moment of solidarity, our world seemed to understand this.

Two of my (Michael's) adult daughters (Emily and Caitlin) are registered nurses who work the COVID-19 unit of our local hospital. Each day they go to work, risking their lives to care for others. They are like masked warrior princesses, battling the virus, who "cure the sick who are there" (Luke 10:9).

Here are three very important lessons from the medical field that church workers helped birth:

1. Many church leaders misunderstand the meaning of "virtual"; it doesn't mean "not real." Some from the Anglo-Catholic persuasion will argue about the efficacy of online communion while others with impulsive worship needs will rush into "in-person worship" (which in aging places like Florida puts vulnerable people in a kill box). Meanwhile, "Virtual Healthcare" is now required curriculum for all incoming medical students, which includes developing competencies in telemedicine, FaceTime, digital communication, virtual clinical interactions, and webside manner.[13]

2. While some churches await theological approval from ivory towers or ecclesiastical overseers, who are insulated from pandemic life in the local congregation, in the medical trenches health care workers are asking what is the optimal pathway to accomplish consensus on core competencies for medical virtualism? Groups of practitioners and experts are starting to self-organize and call for standards of practice in this area. Effective practitioners are being consulted and consensus is coalescing around the need for formally recognized competencies. Thus, we are witnessing the formation of societies who generate consensus around these competencies and develop appropriate training.[14]

3. Let's not forget the "healers" of our minds. A large body of research demonstrates that mental health professionals for over a decade have been effectively using digital technologies to offer psychiatric care, therapy, and online groups. Many of these studies show that these telemental health techniques are shown to be just as effective in the diagnosis and management of various psychiatric conditions as in-person modalities.[15] COVID-19 rapidly accelerated the use of telepsychiatry tools, which had already demonstrated advantages that include "increased care access, enhanced efficiency, reduced stigma associated with visiting mental health clinics, and the ability to bypass diagnosis-specific obstacles to treatment, such as when social anxiety prevents a patient from leaving the house."[16] Telepsychiatry remains challenging because of the need for specific computer skills and access, privacy fears, and of course some cases do require physical contiguity. Yet many mental illnesses can be treated in this way. Further, the pandemic encouraged insurance companies to recognize that these digital means are legitimate and should be covered.

While people in the healing professions have adapted their methods to utilize emerging technologies, overall an aging clergy has been late to the dance. Sadly, it seems like the church is the last place a post-Christendom society turns for healing.

With respect to evangelism, discipleship, and church planting, a diminished understanding of salvation causes these ideas about healing to be disconnected in our minds. The biblical vision of *shalom* (a world at peace) is much more expansive than saving souls for relocation to heaven when they die. It's about God's kingdom breaking into the world now. It's about the healing, renewal, and well-being of the entire cosmos. It's a wholistic vision of God's reign on earth, of which the church is a foretaste. When we understand that evangelism is connected to this greater restoration of individuals, societies, and creation itself, we can break free of the small-minded individualism so prevalent in the Western church.

Evangelism isn't something done to individuals by a specialist; rather like worship, it's a work of the body. Evangelism isn't about extracting people from the world in order to expand the church compound where they can be properly Christianized. It's the work of the Spirit in community with others and it can happen anywhere human beings are connected together. This allows us to open our inner being to the possibility that Jesus goes before us in the technosphere. God is already at work in the lives of those connected by bits and bytes on this digital frontier.

What if cultivating fresh expressions in the digital space is actually a way for us to follow Jesus's commands to "cure the sick who are there" (Luke 10:9)? What if we can become the incarnate presence of Christ in the "space of flows"?

A Theology of Digital Incarnation

One of the ways Christianity thrives in every age is through employing the emerging technological paradigms to foster faithful inculturation. John Dyer writes,

> From Adam's invention of clothing to Edison's invention of the lightbulb, technology is the means by which we transport ourselves to the better worlds we are constantly imagining. The more powerful the tool, the more fully our visions can be realized. When we stumble into a problem we want to solve, we instinctively search for a tool that can help us get from the world with the problem to a world where the problem is solved.[17]

The *Mission-Shaped Church* report from the Church of England in many ways set the trajectory of the Fresh Expressions movement regarding evangelism, discipleship, and church planting (again these are one integrated move for most practitioners). The report highlighted a statement in the foreword of the revised edition of Vincent Donovan's *Christianity Rediscovered.* "Do not try to call them back to where they were, and don't try to call them to where you are, beautiful as that place may seem to you. You must have the courage to go with them to a place where neither you nor they have been before."[18]

Regarding *no-longer-Christians* and *not-yet-Christians* in a post-Christendom digital age, how do we go to the place where they are, and go with them on a journey toward Christ? Emerging generations are digital natives and the technosphere is a foreign mission field. They may belong to a different techno-culture than we do. How do we journey into their world? What would incarnational mission look like in the virtual space of the digital age?

Again, we are not advocating that the church should be "digital only." Rather, that in the digital age every church that survives COVID-19 will need to be a blended ecology of analog and digital. There is no supplement for good old, cell-swapping, molecule-exchanging, face-to-face, flesh-and-blood community that "makes our joy complete" (2 John 12). However, we must also take just as seriously the fresh exchange of bits, bytes, and distanced contact mediated through the multitude of digital flows. Real people gather there too. A real community and a real church can form there as well.

And yet, we are not gnostics. We are not arguing for a disembodied spirit-Jesus who was not real flesh and blood, and is not currently enfleshed in his still embodied, resurrected, wound-bearing glorious self. We are actually all about blood and sinew, sweat and stink, incarnation. In fact, a limited understanding of the incarnation has become a stumbling block for church leaders regarding digital church planting, evangelism, and online communion.

One aspect of Jesus's identity is his death-conquering, risen, and embodied self (Col 1:18). However, the New Testament also talks about a Jesus not bound by time and space. A Jesus who passes through walls. A Jesus who is mistaken for a gardener by one of his most faithful disciples (John 20:15). A Jesus who is not recognized until bread is broken and the cup shared (Luke 24:30-31). A Jesus who shows up in blinding light on the road to Damascus (Acts 9:3). And the "Spirit of Jesus" that guides, compels, speaks, and confronts (Acts 16:7). A Jesus who is both one with and distinct from the Holy Spirit (Matt 3:16-17).

We've met that Jesus, personally, not enfleshed in a way that we could place our fingers in the nail holes, like fortunate old Thomas (John 20:27). Michael met that Jesus on the floor of a jail cell in solitary confinement. He spoke, he comforted, he healed, he sent. Roz met Jesus after he got picked up by the cops for stealing. Since his parents tried to ground him for life, Roz jumped at the chance of accepting an invitation to a youth camp from his sister. It was at that camp that Roz encountered Jesus in a way that would change his life.

Were our encounters with Jesus any less real than those first Christians? Is Jesus limited? Can he not show up in any place, at any time, in any form, and any where he chooses?

We think the key struggle here is that the church has confused *incarnation* for *extraction*, in that church can only happen when people gather together physically in a building, usually at a time and place that of course we church people have predetermined, to worship in a way that is appropriate to us. That's all well and good, and very important. But that's not the only way incarnation can happen. There are other forms in which the Spirit takes on flesh among us. There are other forms of *koinonia,* and there always have been from the genesis of our faith.

Obviously, there is a continuing incarnation in the form of the one, holy, catholic, and apostolic church. This visible community, where the word is rightly preached and the sacraments duly administered, is a form of incarnation. It is this gathered community that the Bible calls "body of Christ," "olive tree," "bride of Christ," and so on.

Yet there is another ongoing incarnation of Jesus—the universe itself (Eph 1:23), of which Christ is the Lord, not only the communal dimension, but also the cosmic dimension (Col 1:15-17). Jesus "fills everything" (Eph 4:10). He is not limited to being the head of the church, but is the head of the universe. His living presence has been downloaded into every aspect of creation.

The universe itself is the first incarnation. It is also an ongoing incarnation. It is not a finished product, but is always in the process of becoming creation, re-creation, new creation. Somehow this unfolding incarnation interacts with humanity and our societies and cultures. It is affected by us, responds to us, convicts us, and changes us, as we are affected by the life of Christ filling the world.

We also individually are an ongoing incarnation of Jesus. As Origen said, "What good does it do me if Christ was born in Bethlehem once if he is not born again in my heart through faith?"[19] Every day Christ must be born anew in us. We are all "Christians in the making," in the language of E. Stanley Jones. And as Christians we are a little microcosm of Jesus, in any space where we are, including digital space. We share our life in the divine dance of the Trinity.

So, the idea is ridiculous that Christian community can only happen in a church building, with a professional cleric overseeing the ritual. Analog fresh expressions have been challenging these assumptions for centuries. However, digital forms of new Christian community are an evolving idea in this thinking.

When Jesus died on the cross, the temple veil was torn. In 70 CE the Jerusalem temple, understood as God's primary place of residence on earth, was destroyed. The symbolism of Jesus's death shows us that human beings no longer need to worship God in one location and in one space, neither at Mount Zion nor at Mount Gerizim, for "God is spirit, and it is necessary to worship God in spirit and truth" (John 4:24). We no longer need a middleman, a priest, to access God or make atonement for our sins. That would be the opposite of the "priesthood of all believers," the original design of Jesus's church.

The late Alan Kreider documented the "improbable growth" of the Christian church across the Roman Empire by the millions, with no buildings, no evangelism strategy, and no professional clergy. The early Christians thrived across the known world by how they lived and loved those in the community and those outside of it.

It wasn't until Emperor Constantine, when Christianity became the state religion, that all this changed. Constantine launched massive building projects, supported councils, and catalyzed the clergy caste system. We have often wondered if the church in the United States has been more Constantinian than Christian. Yes, there were benefits, but there were also significant losses.

So now what do we do when we find ourselves in a culture in which physically gathering in buildings is a practice from the past? An insidious lack of relevancy was apparent pre-COVID-19, but it is accelerated by the virus, and the implications of this are far reaching. Returning to packed-out arenas and church buildings is unlikely for many areas in our country.

The "word became flesh and made his home among us" (John 1:14). Would it be too much of a stretch to imagine that the "Word became bits and bytes" and made its home among us? Is the incarnation of Jesus limited to the space of place, or is the spirit of Jesus at work in the space of flows as well? What would it look like for Christians to *tabernacle* in digital space? What would it look like for us to "take on" digitization to form community with those outside the reach of analog forms of church (Phil 2)?

Jesus himself used the tools of his day. He adopted the trade of being a *tekton,* someone who used tools to create with the sin-broken materials of earth. Think of the technology of cross (the most horrible tool of humiliation and punishment known to the ancient world) and city (itself a convergence of technologies). And even in his resurrected state, he used the technology of the day, "a charcoal fire," to make breakfast for the disciples (John 21:9).

The Iconoclast Controversy simmered for centuries over the question, "Can we make images that represent Jesus?" Isn't that both some kind of violation of the commandment not to make graven images and a form of idolatry?

John of Damascus was considered the leading theologian of that era, and he wrote,

> When the Invisible One becomes visible to flesh then you may draw a likeness of His form. When He who is pure spirit, without form or limit, immeasurable in the boundlessness of His own nature, existing as God, takes upon Himself the form of a servant in substance and in

stature, and a body of flesh, then you may draw His likeness, and show it to anyone willing to contemplate it.[20]

The early church decided that images of Jesus were themselves a manifestation of the wonder of the incarnation. The art of making images of Jesus was a miniature re-incarnation of Jesus. Even portrayals of Jesus that were marred and twisted amply illustrate the profound mystery of the God who put on flesh. Images of Jesus theologically reinforce this "word made flesh" God.[21]

Perhaps what we are doing when we take on bits and bytes in the cyberspace of netizens from across the world is not much different than those icon-making artists. They were using the advanced technologies and tools of their day to create renderings of Jesus that drew people into a state of worship. While idols point away from God, icons point people to God. Our technologies can accomplish both. But when we seek to form fresh expressions through our digital tools, we converge in a pixelated mosaic of grace. We become an icon pointing to God. Even a Jesus community imperfectly formed can accomplish this.

It is our Christian heritage to use the technological forces of the day for the expansion of the church. The church was formed in the technologies of its own social milieu. This is the consistent legacy of Christians across the ages. We form communities of healing and shalom in every space and place of creation. When we do this, we become the little dots that when connected together form an icon of Jesus.

Discipleship Matrix: Societies, Classes, Bands, and Visitation Remixed

Early Methodism was one of the greatest renewal movements in the history of the church. In *A Field Guide to Methodist Fresh Expressions*, we reflected on how the Fresh Expressions movement is a remixed Methodism for the twenty-first century. The book traced how Wesley used the emerging societal restructuring of the dawning industrial age and

89

synthesized multiple technologies and ecclesial innovations to catalyze a movement. A major focus 250 years later is rethinking what the "fields" look like in the network society and how "field preaching" is a key strategy.

People awakened in the fields were connected in a life of discipleship through societies, classes, and bands. Wesleyans describe discipleship as a journey or simply the "way of salvation." This is a journey of God's grace often experienced in primarily three waves: (1) **prevenient**: the grace that goes before us, preceding our conscious awareness that the Spirit is wooing us, beckoning us to embrace God's free offer of salvation in Christ; (2) **justifying**: as our hearts and lives are changed (metanoia), the Spirit dwells within us in an intensely personal way; and (3) **sanctifying**: God is working within us to accomplish a complete restoration resulting in a new creation, going on the way toward perfection in love.

Evangelism and discipleship are inextricably linked in the Wesleyan theological system. John Wesley spoke of responding to these waves of grace in terms of: (1) **awakening**: one hears the gospel and responds to prevenient grace; (2) **belief**: the faithful commitment to change our lives in response to justifying grace; and (3) **holiness**: a lifelong journey of growth in sanctifying grace. It was possible for one to move forward and backward in these stages.

Typically, "field preaching" catalyzed the "awakening" stage in a new believer's life (although Wesley reports repentance and conversion were common as well). But for Wesley, simply "awakening" people through field preaching and not connecting them to a discipleship process was "begetting children for the slaughter."[22]

For each of the waves of grace, there were corresponding forums to connect people to that grace. As to represent prevenient grace, Wesley used the united societies. To promote justifying grace, he developed the class meeting. To advance sanctifying grace, he emphasized the bands.

Religious societies didn't originate with Wesley. In the 1670s there was a growing sense of need for renewal in the Anglican church. Societies were small, but groups of serious Christians gathered together for Bible study, mutual edification, and prayer. The leaders in the Church of England limited membership in *religious societies* to members of the Church of England. The Methodist societies were a more inclusive version of these religious societies of the day. Anyone was able to participate, Christian or not; the only

90

requirement was "a desire to flee wrath to come." Some societies were as small as twenty people, others grew to several hundred people. These discipleship forums were a place where participants met together for prayer, worship, preaching, fellowship, and spiritual direction. They watched over one another in love as they journeyed from grace to grace.

The class meeting was an essential component of the Methodist movement. Class meetings provided accountability in a smaller, more conversational and personal forum, where people could honestly discuss "how goes it with your soul?" Usually, class meetings were mixed groups of men and women, typically about seven to twelve members, organized according to geography. These were people who typically had experienced justification by faith and were seeking to grow in grace, but people at different levels of spiritual maturity participated in the class meeting together. Class leaders also regularly provided exhortation of the word.[23]

Bands consisted of smaller groups of four to six people of the same gender and marital status. This cell offered a more intimate communal space for those who were seeking to live a life of holiness. While people at different stages participated in the class meetings, bands were for those "going onto perfection." These were mature disciples experiencing sanctifying grace, which involved the regular confession of sin and healing (James 5:16). This was a forum for authentic and searching conversations. Penitent bands were a variation in which believers who backslid into sin could experience spiritual rehabilitation. Bands were also a place for the proclamation of scripture and testimony.[24]

The small-group system was the engine that drove the Methodist movement. The matrix required an army of faithful disciples to grow and sustain, which unleashed one of the most powerful examples of a lay-led renewal movement in human history. Laity preached in the fields, as well as led the societies, classes, and bands. Both men and women served in leadership together, another innovation for this time. Methodists saw within this matrix a revival comparable to the early church. It was a powerful system of multiplication, which took people through a journey from being "awakened" to leading and discipling others.

Jack Jackson suggests an often-neglected facet of Wesley's "evangelistic vision," which is an integral component of this matrix: *visitation*. Jackson shows that Wesley saw visiting from "house to house," by clergy and laity alike, as the prescription for Methodism's vitality. Late in Wesley's ministry, in laying out a plan for the thriving of Methodism in Scotland, he provided three keys: (1) preaching abroad as much as possible (field preaching), (2) traveling to every possible town and village, and (3) visiting each member of the society at home.[25]

The one-on-one, personal, direct, and searching conversation in the group provided the forum for intense spiritual examination. Wesley trained Methodists to meet people's physical needs first, then their spiritual needs. This wholistic idea of "healing the sick" is the understated revolutionary power of the Methodist revival. This personal and private relational exchange couldn't be accomplished in field preaching or even in the small-group system. Here, through visitation, was the private space where holiness could be truly nurtured. Yet this intimate conversational forum was also a place of proclamation. Jackson writes, "The proclamation that began in the fields continued in societies, became more pointed in classes, and was most personal in visitation."[26]

A connection between personal visitation and apprenticeship can flesh out what this matrix looks like on the new missional frontier.

Hollinghurst, in his thorough study of mission-shaped evangelism in post-Christendom society, describes three repeating stages in the most effective projects: (1) build relationships in the wider community on the territory of those we are trying to reach; (2) create or find places where Christians and non-Christians build relationships and explore issues and questions of lifestyle, faith, and spirituality on neutral territory, together; and (3) establish discipleship groups explicitly aimed at those who want to explore the Christian faith.[27]

As practitioners and students of fresh expressions for the past decade, we find these three simple stages to be on target. Further, it's not hard to see the correlations between these stages and the evangelism-discipleship matrix of early Methodism: (1) field preaching has the character of building relationships in the space of our other, yet the form of proclamation must shift to the "sermonic conversation" described in Download 7; (2) societies very much reflect the nature of fresh expressions in which people at varying stages of spiritual development do life together around a common passion; and (3) classes and bands represent the smaller break-out and opt-in groups that develop alongside fresh expressions.

Yet we would add an additional layer of one-on-one relationships emphasized by Jackson in visitation. These are the apprenticeships that form organically between mature disciples and the newly awakened in these fresh expressions.

Here are some diagrams to illustrate what we mean.

Diagram 1 conceptualizes the discipleship matrix of early Methodism, including each forum, and the corresponding spiritual stage:

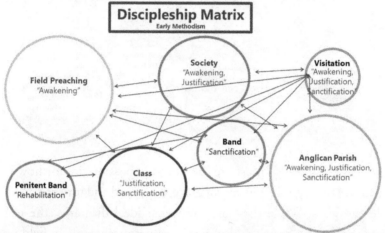

Diagram 2 illustrates the blended ecology discipleship matrix for incarnational mission in the digital age, including each forum, and the corresponding spiritual stage:

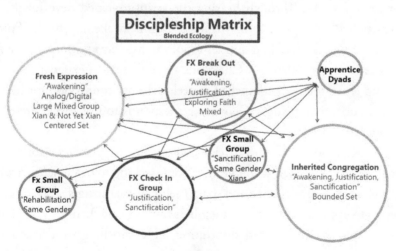

Diagram 3 illustrates an actual existing fresh expression of Wildwood UMC and how the blended ecology discipleship matrix works, including each forum, and the corresponding spiritual stage:

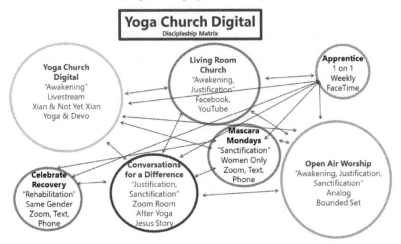

The diagrams also illustrate the multiple possibilities for how people may move through the journey of grace, backward and forward, with multiple pathways. While these are somewhat ideal diagrams, the reality is always quite a bit messier. Also, just as sometimes people in field preaching gatherings could experience awakening, justification, or movement toward sanctification, so the forums do not limit how the Spirit may move.

For instance, let's say Tricia has been coming to Yoga Church Digital for several weeks. Through hearing the scripture-based devotionals, integrated with the practice of yoga, she begins awakening to the Spirit's prevenient work. She then decides to join in for conversations with a difference in Zoom. There, as Christians share their own experience of following Jesus, she feels compelled to seek a deeper connection for herself. She attends Living Room Church and responds to the gospel presented through the Jesus story.

Karen follows up with Tricia, inviting her to Mascara Mondays, a small group of women who join by Zoom, seeking to be "sanctified while single" as they drink coffee and share their spiritual struggles. Tricia really begins to appreciate one of the members of the group, Laura. When Laura shares, her spirituality and disposition are compelling to Tricia. Laura and Tricia agree to meet weekly by FaceTime. Laura begins to take Tricia through the six-step process outlined in the "App It" section below.

Their group sends each other prayers and encouraging Bible passages throughout the week. Eventually Tricia visits Open Air Worship, the analog worship experience that meets outdoors. After some period of initial spiritual growth and excitement, Tricia begins drinking with a group of friends and has a random sexual encounter with a man she hardly knows. Laura suggests that she try the women's small group Celebrate Recovery (CR) Zoom meeting.

In CR, Tricia discovers she isn't alone in her struggles. She finds safety, accountability, and support. As she grows in her relationship with Christ, Tricia decides to turn her passion for painting into a fresh expression of her own. She gathers a group of friends on Zoom, reads a couple verses of scripture, offers a devotional and prayer, and they paint together. As the community grows, she decides to provide an "opt in" conversations for a difference of her own. Now she is helping women go through the same journey of grace that she had made for herself.

While this is a hypothetical and composite story, we have seen versions of this narrative occur repeatedly. While each person may interact with each forum differently, and move at their own pace, you can see how the whole ecosystem creates a discipleship matrix that facilitates a movement through awakening, discipleship, and church planting. All of this can occur primarily through these digital mediums.

How can we continue to sustain a healthy mix between digital and analog? How do we cultivate these new Christian communities in digital space? To these questions we now turn.

App It

Chat Box

Gather with your team physically or digitally and discuss the following questions.

Discipleship Covenant

We believe that a replicable discipleship process must be so simple that any believer can do it. At Wildwood we have adapted the Twelve Steps to provide a six-step framework where someone can move through the journey of grace. People pair up in discipleship dyads. The disciple serves as a guide to walk alongside the apprentice through the journey of grace.

Discipleship Covenant

Covenant: A relationship with clear boundaries.

God often offers relationships through covenants: Adamic Covenant Genesis 1:26-30; 2:16-17, Noahic Covenant Genesis 9:11, Abrahamic Covenant Genesis 12:1-3, Palestinian Covenant Deuteronomy 30:1-10, Mosaic Covenant Deuteronomy 11, Davidic Covenant 2 Samuel 7:8-16, New Covenant Jeremiah 31:31-34, Matthew 26:28, Hebrews 9:15. The new covenant is cut into the heart muscle, a blood bond between Jesus and his followers.

I _____ am covenanting to enter into a relationship of total transparency with_____
_____.

My desire in this relationship is to grow as an apprentice of Jesus. I am seeking to "love the Lord your God with all your heart, and with all your soul, and with all your mind . . . and love your neighbor as yourself" (Matt 22:37-40). I want to live a life ripe with the "fruits of the Spirt" "love, joy, peace, patience, kindness, generosity, faithfulness, gentleness, and self-control" (Gal 5:22-23).

I will follow this process outlined in Scripture:

1. Surrender (to a covenantal apprentice relationship). "Follow me as I follow Christ" (1 Cor 11:1).

2. Inventory (examination of our souls). "Carry your cross . . . who does not first sit down and estimate the cost" (Luke 14:25-32).

3. Confession (for full transparency and healing). "Confess your sins one to another and be healed" (Jas 5:16).

4. Amends (a guided process of righting wrongs). "If you remember your brother has something against you, leave your gift there in front of the altar. First go and be reconciled to your brother" (Matt 5:23-24).

5. Cultivating Christoformity (ongoing inventory, confession, spiritual practices, and check-ins with discipler). "For those whom He foreknew, He also predestined to become conformed to the image of His Son" (Rom 8:29).

6. Disciple Others (take others through the journey). "Go therefore and make disciples of all nations, baptizing them in the name of the Father and of the Son and of the Holy Spirit, and teaching them to obey everything that I have commanded you" (Matt 28:18-20).

Signed_____ Date_____

While this covenant is contextually appropriate for Wildwood and not a universal prescription, might you use this question to have a conversation about:

How are we moving people along the journey from repentance to sharing their faith with others?

What would a covenant look like for us to provide relational boundaries for discipling relationships?

E-haviors

Consider how these practices might be helpful as missionaries in the digital age.

Most of our e-haviors have been focused on what to do in digital space. Here we want to suggest that these be balanced with spiritual disciplines in analog.

1. **Tech fasting**: Go away for periods of non-tech times. Take a tech Sabbath. Don't worry, the madness will be waiting when you return! Physically remove tech devices if you need to.

2. **Use scheduled posts**: Rather than posting whatever thought comes into your mind, prayerfully think through what you are communicating. Save your thoughts and schedule opportune times to post.

3. **Remove all devices out of bedroom at a fixed time at night**: Screen time before bed disrupts the ability to fall asleep and the sleep cycle. Charge your device in another room. Make them less accessible. Never allow children to have devices in their bedrooms.

4. **No social media till high school**: There has been quite a bit of research on how destructive technology can be for young children. The natural development of their brains and social skills can be damaged by too much access too early. A good rule of thumb is no social media till high school.

5. **Work out a time budget with your kid, let them lead the way:** Most children will appreciate an upfront conversation about the dangers of technology and appropriate boundaries. Let them help you shape a plan that works around their scheduled screen times.

6. **Ban all digital devices from meetings:** The best digital missionaries ban technology from important meetings of staff and leadership. These devices distract from and impede the process of a good meeting.

Livestream: Samuel Hubbard

Hey y'all, this is Sam Hubbard coming to you from the bayous of Louisiana. I'm the associate director for the Office of Congregation Development and Transformation for the Louisiana Annual Conference of The United Methodist Church. Or, in ordinary language, I help people plant churches. As a church planter myself, nothing gives me more joy than going to new places to reach new people with Jesus's life-changing message.

It doesn't really get better than that. (Well . . . unless it's a shrimp and roast beef po-boy . . . hoo-wee!)

It's no secret that planting churches is hard. (If it were easy, everyone would be doing it.) However, planting a church in today's post-Christian world makes things even harder. Then, throw in civil unrest, natural disasters, and . . . oh yeah . . . A GLOBAL PANDEMIC . . . all in the same year, and it becomes, well . . . VIRTUALLY IMPOSSIBLE.

Our office began working with Pastor Fernie Rivera in 2017. Fernie is a planter through and through, and after participating in a church plant in Chicago, he moved to Baton Rouge, Louisiana, to do what a planter does: start new churches. After helping to launch and lead a new worship community in Baton Rouge, Fernie felt the Spirit lead him to Mid-City. Mid-City is an area of Baton Rouge that is economically and ethnically diverse. After several months of exploring and engaging with the people of Mid-City, while working with the leadership of First United Methodist Church-Baton Rouge and our office, the vision of Mid-City Church was born.

As with most new church plants, Fernie did the usual things a church planter does. Leadership and worship teams were formed, marketing was done, strategies and systems were created, studies and curriculums were developed, and the official launch day of Mid-City Church (MCC) was scheduled for March 15, 2020. It was going to be HUGE! That was until our leaders here in Louisiana placed quarantine protocols in effect to slow the spread of COVID-19 on March 13, 2020, thus canceling the big launch of MCC.

Mid-City Church, like every church, scrambled to adjust. Mid-City Church offered worship online, gathered in small groups over Zoom, and assembled small teams that cared and served the Mid-City community they loved so much. However, everybody was asking, "when will MCC launch?" (I mean, a church isn't really a church until it has a massive launch with more than two hundred people, and a bunch of buzz, right?) This question began to weigh heavily on our office, on Fernie, and the community of MCC.

Then one day, during a coaching call, we were having a tough conversation about MCC. (If you're a planter or coach, you know what those calls are like . . . no Bueno.) As we started going through the numbers, we began to see something. MCC had more than sixty people in small groups . . . not affinity groups or supper clubs, but discipling groups. Those groups were super-diverse and super-young, one of them being all Hispanic musicians. Most of them have never been or had left the church, and all of them were giving and serving sacrificially.

When we were looking at these numbers, we realized MCC had already launched, and it had launched BIG! Fernie has launched a digital church that is growing, alive, and reaching new people in new places. (MCC even has members in Houston!) Now, this has opened our eyes to new possibilities. Now that MCC's digital campus has launched successfully, it is preparing for its second campus, its first physical location. Mid-City Church is also praying and preparing to launch a Hispanic community, its third campus. This was all done in fewer than twelve-months, during a pandemic, without physically meeting. Mid-City Church has shown us that when it comes to church planting, everything is VIRTUALLY POSSIBLE.

Cultivating Digital Fresh Expressions

H ere we download a process for cultivating fresh expressions of church and share some real stories of what it looks like.

The Loving First Journey

Michael Moynagh and Michael Beck lay out what they call the "loving first cycle" in their book *The 21st Century Christian: Following Jesus Where Life Happens*. The journey describes how most new Christian communities seem to emerge. We briefly summarize here how the journey can serve as the process to cultivate digital fresh expressions of church.

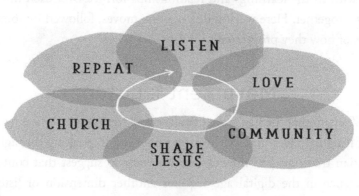

It's this simple, really:

- find a friend (or several) in some area of your life,
- prayerfully discover a simple way to love the people in your relational network,
- deepen relationships with them in an intentional way,
- share your faith in Jesus when opportunities present themselves, and
- encourage those coming to faith to form a small Christian community where they are, and connect them to the wider church.

Of course, we know this process is messier in practice than in theory. We can't think of this as a neat linear process. It's easier to understand this in the metaphor of a journey in which there is a progression of moves. Sometimes on a journey you have to take an unexpected turn, take a detour, or do a total U-turn! And this is true of the loving first cycle as well.

For the most part, the journey of forming new Christian community will happen in some sequence of these stages. We are trying to avoid the language of steps or stages, as it is a tendency of the church to try and create the "just add water and stir" recipes for success.

Perhaps it's most helpful to think of these moves as another leg of the journey. We turn the corner only to find the next wonderful vista on the horizon. But each move precedes from and flows into the next. We never stop "listening" and "loving," as we make the journey toward church. We carry with us the learnings and relationships formed over each mile that we take together. Here we will describe the moves, followed by some real stories of how they progressed.

Movement 1: Listen

We claim that the first stage of cultivating fresh expressions is a double act of listening. This involves hearing what God is speaking through *both* Christian tradition *and* the culture. We want to suggest that contextual intelligence in the digital age requires another dimension of listening.

This question could be our guide: "What technology is connecting these people here?" This question expands into a process of triple listening: to God through church tradition, to God in the physical space, and to God in the digital space. Missionaries do all three processes.

This process will require your team to spend time in prayer together, studying scripture together, sharing about what you hear God saying, and keeping that in conversation with the wider tradition of the church. Equally, you will need to prayerfully inhabit the analog and digital spaces where God is calling you to join into what the Spirit is up to. Incarnational mission requires you to actually be present with the people, in their places, joining in their common practices.

Listening involves learning the local language, customs, assumptions, hopes, and dreams. It requires seeking to understand their customs, rituals, and values. What do they watch? What do they listen to? What is their pain? What is good news to them? What is their belief system? How does all this intersect with the gospel of Jesus Christ?

One benefit of the digital ecosystem is the ability to ask a large group of people about its needs, challenges, and hopes. With the internet came the phenomenon of "crowdsourcing." This is typically understood as a sourcing model in which we can obtain goods and services from a large, open, and quickly evolving group of participants. Teams across many fields are now using crowdsourcing to organize and divide work between participants to achieve a cumulative result.

Followers of Jesus can use this same approach, but rather than toward a consumeristic end, we can seek to genuinely know, love, and serve the netizens in our relational networks. For example, I (Michael) started a new appointment to a declining congregation in July of 2020. In the height of the pandemic spreading in Florida, an epicenter of the virus, I was unable to employ my usual methods. While I visited the existing members in a series of virtual home visits, I also used the simple "looking for recommendations" feature of my personal Facebook profile. I asked, "Dear Ocala friends, what are the greatest challenges, needs, and concerns in the city and surrounding area?" People began to respond with things like COVID-19, food insecurity, racism, and so on. I then invited all those who responded to have a town-hall gathering we called a "Community Listening Session." This led to the creation of several fresh expressions, described at the end of this download.

Part of our double listening will always include discovering the fragmentation and the pain people are experiencing. God is always at work in the gaps. Listening always involves three simple dimensions: (1) prayer (staying in communication with God), (2) observation (attending to the details of the virtual or physical ecosystem), and (3) encounter (leaving room to have conversations with the people we meet.

As we go out in teams, sent by Jesus, we become the answer to our own prayers (Luke 10:2). In this posture of wonder and listening we discover our *person of peace*. This is the person who calls our new frontiers simply "home." We come into this relationship in a place of vulnerability. We are dependent on their hospitality. We are the guest; they are the host. They welcome us and grant us access, as in password login credentials for this relational network. Once we have been granted access, our job is simply to *love*, through eating, staying, and healing together (Luke 10).

Movement 2: Love

David Augsburger famously said, "Being heard is so close to being loved that for the average person, they are almost indistinguishable."[1] Love flows organically as we sincerely desire to be present and listen to people. Loving is not about doing something for or to a group of people who need what we have but is a mutual exchange of blessing. There is no hidden agenda. We can't see "love" as a vehicle to "plant a church." Love is the end. Love is the goal. Love is the way. Sometimes fresh expressions will form from our loving of others; sometimes they won't. In other words, love is all about the messy work of building relationships.

The danger of hyperconnectivity is isolation. Although we can be in communication with people across the world at the speed of digital light, many of those relationships seem superficial and fragile. We scroll through our friends list and find some have decided to unfriend us. We look to our Twitter or Instagram accounts and discover our followers have decreased. Then we wonder what we said or did to alienate people we once shared a connection with. The old cliché, "easy come, easy go," is certainly true in the digital age. But can followers of Jesus embody a transfiguring narrative amidst this reality?

The first Christians embodied a distinct countercultural *habitus* (a system of schemes of thought, perception, appreciation, and action). We like to describe this as the *Jesus habitus*. Those first disciples were called followers of "the way" of Jesus. This first earned them the title "Christians," meaning "little Christs." With no evangelism campaign, no professional clergy, and no dedicated buildings, the faith grew by the millions for three hundred years across the Roman Empire. It grew primarily through how the early followers lived this distinct habitus in a world often hostile to their faith. They were known by their love. So again, in the vast cyberscape of the digital age, we live out a distinct, countercultural way of following Jesus.

In some cases, our behaviors, grounded in the self-emptying, sacrificial love of Christ, will need to be the exact opposite of a "selfie generation." In a culture where idols of bits and bytes are on every digital corner, we need to be icons that point to God. For us, the answer to Facebook's feed prompt, "What's on your mind?" should be, "if anything is excellent and if anything is admirable, focus your thoughts on these things: all that is true, all that is holy, all that is just, all that is pure, all that is lovely, and all that is worthy of praise" (Phil 4:8). We can be curators of goodness, beauty, and truth, pointing to how God is at work in it all. We can find ways to turn that question around into a posture of listening, inviting netizens to tell us "what's on *your* mind" rather than constantly telling them what's on *ours*. We can invite people to pray, converse, and ponder the mystery of God. We can model appropriate civil discourse without attacking and polarizing those who think differently than we do.

It's imperative that we establish this call to "heal" on the foundation of building meaningful relationships. We are welcomed in, doing life together, and there is a kind of healing that takes place.

Movement 3: Community

As we listen and love, real relationships form. In Luke 10:7, a posture of abiding, "Remain in this house, eating and drinking whatever they set before you. . . . Don't move from house to house." This idea of sharing life, breaking bread, and being the church in the places where life happens is prominent in Jesus's missional blueprint. What does community look like in the space of flows? Can we really have the kind of *koinonia* the Bible describes in a digital medium?

Sherry Turkle, in *Alone Together*, questions this assumption: "Communities are places where one feels safe enough to take the good and the bad. In communities, others come through for us in hard times, so we are willing to hear what they have to say, even if we don't like it." She reminds us that community literally means "to give among each other."[2]

Turkle thinks of the digital ecosystem as a "third place," a concept that originated with Ray Oldenburg and is used heavily within the Fresh Expressions movement. Yet she ultimately decided that the convenient nature of fast-friends in cyberspace, friends easily made and easily lost, didn't hold up to the classic understanding of community. She writes, "Communities are constituted by physical proximity, shared concerns, real consequences, and common responsibilities."[3]

The kind of community envisioned in scripture is defined as *koinonia* (transliterated form of the Greek word (κοινωνια), which refers to communion, interpenetration, fellowship, and sharing in a jointly contributed gift (Phil 2:1). The character of Christian community therefore is the most intimate of terms, quite literally "intercourse," a deep and unbreakable relational bond.

A very challenging question is whether *koinonia* exists in most traditional analog congregations. McDonaldization describes the kind of rationalization of production, work, and consumption that rose to prominence in the late-twentieth century. The "franchised" church can be compared to an assembly line in which professional clergy oversee an organization that provides religious goods and services. On Sundays, members come to pick up their spiritual Happy Meals and then go about the week.

This highly consumer-oriented version of church is particularly prevalent in denominations as well as in the independent evangelical churches. People chose churches based on what most effectively meets their own needs. They are looking for a comfortable kind of worship, preaching, or youth and children's program. If those services fail to meet expectations, they will try another church. This phenomenon of "church shopping" is actually an unintended growth strategy for many congregations. If we do our programs with more "excellence" than the church down the road, we will attract the practicing Christians in the neighborhood.

When we apply the critique about "authentic community" to analog congregations, it leads to these deeper questions.

It's harder for digital immigrants to envision whether this kind of community could be possible through digital means. However, COVID-19 may have challenged some of our assumptions. When the only kind of community available is digitally enabled, how do our relationships fair? Is it producing or establishing *koinonia?*

For the authors, we decided independently that during the pandemic we should increase the frequency of connection time with our core leaders. We met weekly on Zoom, as well as sending frequent texts, phone calls, emails, and connecting through FaceTime. We both discovered that using these technologies bound us together in even deeper ways. We leaned into this digitally enabled connection and came out of quarantine bound more firmly through a common bond.

During the period of this writing, we (Roz and Michael) never actually met physically. Yet we have a very close and real relationship. We have connected at a soul level through sharing stories and confessions. We have taught students, planted churches, offered webinars, and written this book together, enabled entirely through digital means.

I (Michael) have deep and abiding relationships that are completely digital in nature with mentors and friends across the country. I also participate in a covenant group, a band of brothers, fellow clergy deeply embedded in the challenges of pastoring in a sharply declining denomination. As we are spread across the southern United States (one of us is an army chaplain), our relationships have been formed and sustained mostly through digital means.

As we will propose later, a remixed system of societies, classes, and bands is enabled through these digital flows. In our band meetings, which are gender specific, men with men, women with women, some of the deepest forms of repentance, confession, and healing take place. In fact, we discovered some people are far more comfortable sharing intimate details of their lives in the safety of their own homes, connected to their band digitally. Zoom rooms can be just as holy a space as the confessional in the cavernous sanctuary. We are sustaining a level of authentic community that is not disposable with a click of the mouse.

It is through the repeated patterns of loving-withness that community forms. Relationships gain strength over time, and trust begins to build among the group.

A profound sense of connectedness begins to form, as we gather in digitally connected rooms. The community becomes life-giving as we experience the healing of our isolation. There is no question for us that the relationships we formed through online spaces are real. This is not "virtual," as in a simulation of the real; this is "real virtuality." We found belonging, connected together by the Holy Spirit, flowing through our distanced contact. As community forms and we wrestle with the mountain top and valley experiences of doing life, opportunities unfold to share our faith.

Movement 4: Share Jesus

In Luke 10:1-9, God's kingdom (a real virtuality) accompanies healing, eating, and abiding together. This need not be an intimidating thing; it happens just as naturally as our conversations evolve into meaningful sharing about real struggles. As we stated from the beginning, evangelism is not a distinct work area for Christian specialists; it is the work of the whole people of God.

Evangelism, discipleship, and church planting are not programs, departments, or the expertise of specialists, or even of entrepreneurs. They are a single movement of the Spirit that flows through the life of every believer. No person who has experienced the grace and love of Christ could ever keep that to themselves. The essence of being a Christian is re-presenting Christ to those we encounter in our daily lives. We come to faith, grow in our faith, and share our faith in one continuous life rhythm.

When sharing faith in the midst of authentic relationships, the community grows in depth and strength. When Jesus is the center of a community, the community can sustain all kinds of challenges. We move beyond whatever passion, hobby, practice, or social affinity the community has formed around. The activities that we share in together are anchored in Christ.

Koinonia is a concept encompassing this shared belief, or even a willingness to believe, in each other that helps create the depth and intimacy of relationship. For instance, consider Twelve-Step recovery programs, such as Alcoholics Anonymous, Narcotics Anonymous, Al Anon, Sexaholics Anonymous, and so on. These groups employ the term *fellowship* in ways closer to the biblical concept than some churches do. People are bound together by an honest confession of their brokenness and a willingness to believe in a higher power. They have found a new community in which to do life.

In these fellowships, we go through a journey (the Twelve Steps) that takes us through the steps of powerlessness, coming to believe, confession, amends, spiritual enlargement, and sharing the message with others. If this sounds biblical, it's because it is. Bill W. and Dr. Bob, cofounders of Alcoholics Anonymous (AA), took the spiritual principles of the *Oxford Group* (a Christian organization first known as the *First Century Christian Fellowship* founded by Lutheran priest Frank Buchman in 1921) and codified and expanded its tenets.

Alcoholics Anonymous uses a communal technology called the "open meeting" to provide a safe gathering space for alcoholics seeking recovery. The central idea is an entire psychic change, which can be experienced through working the Twelve Steps. Having had a spiritual awakening as the results of the steps, members of the community commit to carry that message to all who still suffer from the disease. Alcoholics Anonymous practices a "belonging before believing" approach to forming community. The only requirement to join is a "desire to stop drinking."

While the program suggests no specific religion, faith in a "higher power" and ongoing growth is the "solution" to the mental, physical, and spiritual malady of addiction. One goes through this process as an apprentice to a guide, called a "sponsor." The sponsor takes their sponsee through the same process that the sponsor went through. In our opinion, "fellowships" like this are one of the greatest discipleship programs in the world. They take people through a journey of faith in which they are spiritually transformed.

One could say that recovery fellowships are more faithful to Jesus's design for the church than the church itself.

When COVID-19 struck, these anonymous fellowships were forced into the wonderful world of Zoom as well. I (Michael), myself a part of these fellowships, found my recovery meetings now also taking place in the digital flows. After several weeks of people trying to figure out how to use the technology, we fell into a rhythm in which these digital rooms became the new normal. I still participate in these fellowships digitally and find them more meaningful.

At this simplest level, a disciple is a learner. We equate discipleship with learning to become a "little Christ," the root meaning of the term *Christian*. Discipleship involves being mentored by Jesus in community with other Christians. We grow together in the Jesus *habitus*, more and more taking on his heart, way, and life.

The discipleship process involves sharing our faith with others in community. It's not simply the job of the program director or the church pastor. Discipleship is a communal endeavor; it is a work of the whole people of God. Again, evangelism, discipleship, and church planting are entwined.

A church risks losing its passion when breaking out this work in specializations and programs. Sharing our faith becomes intimidating, and the needs of specially gifted or professional persons get in the way of the momentum. Jesus doesn't pass on the Great Commission (Matt 28:18-20) or the Great Commandment (John 13:34) to a select group of disciples but to the whole church. If sharing our faith has become so complicated that every single believer isn't confident and comfortable doing so, we've suboptimized Jesus's guidance for the church.

A group of young seminary graduates once told one of us, "evangelism is archaic and not part of my calling." Perhaps they, too, are reacting to a caricature of the traveling, crusading evangelist. However, a dismissive attitude toward faith sharing is a teachable moment. If sharing the faithfulness of Jesus is not something fundamental to the calling of every believer, we become something other than the body of Christ.

In the digital flows, the playing field is leveled. Each believer can be a part of God's ever-expanding kingdom. Leaders are discovering that digital mediums involve simple ways to reach into their relational sphere, as simple as sending friend invites to a gathering, emailing a link to our Zoom gathering, creating a group on Meetup.com, posting a YouTube video that highlights what we do, and so on.

Remember that God is already virtually at work in every life. We don't bring God with us. We are joining into what God is already doing in the intersection of our relationships. A "belonging before believing" mode of evangelism isn't about racking up "decisions for Christ." We are simply growing in our relationships with God and each other, sharing our faith mutually when the time is appropriate. We join Jesus in the digital ecosystem, befriending, chatting, and doing life together as we go along. As we do this together, we are moving into the next leg of the journey—*ecclesia* or simply *church*.

Movement 5: Church

Journeying together through the flows in our daily networks centered on shared practices can force us to reconsider our inherited definitions of church. We expand from this small idea of church as a building that we go into from time to time. We are already part of a community or network that expands across the digital ecosystem. Church isn't merely what happens when we gather in one particular locale, but also when we are scattered across a mobilized, digitally-enabled culture. This dual mode of being church has been present since the beginning (Acts 11, 15)—a church gathered and scattered, collected and distributed, Jerusalem and Antioch, deep roots and wild branches (Rom 11). We could think of each of the spaces where community can form as habitats in a digital ecosystem.

Some of the people participating in our fresh expressions gather in several of them, not just one. During certain seasons at Wildwood, church was happening somewhere (tattoo parlor, dog park, Moe's Southwest Grill, yoga studio, Martin Luther King Jr. Center, the runners track, and so on) almost every day of the week. These micro-communities network with each other and people try different gatherings they think they might like.

This migration continued throughout the pandemic outbreak but in a different way. Every day there was some Zoom room, Facebook group, or Meetup, gathering in a digital place. People in different places along their spiritual journey were connecting, encouraging others, swapping ideas. Apprenticeships were formed naturally, and people began to meet over FaceTime or via text between gatherings. The church is now spread across the network, using digital flows to connect, gather, pray, and worship.

There is a *oneness* to this church, unified by the common center, which is Jesus himself. There is a *holiness* to this church because people are authentically sharing their struggles and leaning into the power from God for transformation. There is a *catholicity* to this church because it's connected across space and time through digital means and is staying in conversation with the wider church tradition. There is a *sentness* to this church, spilling out across the digital landscape, engaging people right in the place where they spend most of their time. This community embodies what the early Christian creeds affirm as the "marks of the church," that it is one, holy, catholic, and apostolic.

While each of these gatherings may be in different stages of development, some include sermonic conversations, intentional worship, and sacraments. These too were enabled by digital means. We know we are on disputed ground here with virtual sacraments. I (Michael) address this in a persuasive essay, "A Missional Meal: The Digital Practice of the Lord's Supper,"[4] by engaging scripture, tradition, reason, and experience to make a case for the practice of online communion.

However, let's think about this from another angle. We enjoy a fun, hypothetical breakout session with our students. Say that Elon Musk and SpaceX plan to build a Mars settlement, and that it has recently made headlines: "A Million Humans Could Live on Mars By the 2060s."[5]

Now, say that John, a colonist on Mars, has an encounter with Jesus. He is the first Christian on the planet.

1. He wants to be baptized into the faith. How will we facilitate this?

2. He wants to take Holy Communion. How will this work?

3. Are his relationships with Jesus and the church real?

We ask our students how they would respond to these questions. Then the fun begins! We have never had a single student make the case that we need to fly an ordained priest to Mars, including students from the highest sacramental church traditions. It's always about how to facilitate community through the digital medium, so that John can become the first convert in the Mars colony, and start evangelizing to plant a new church on the planet!

Yet when it comes to online communion and baptism on this planet, our imaginations are not at full capacity. We immediately default to the clericalism and control over mediation that has diminished the church for so long.

Nevertheless, on this new missional frontier, the old strategies focused solely on physical locations are incapable of reaching the growing share of netizens.

Movement 6: Repeat

This final move is important. Repeating is not just about starting all over; it's about multiplication. We are cultivating little Christian communities, like satellites orbiting a physical center. As people come to faith, they are empowered by the Spirit to share Jesus in a way that's unique to them and their affinities, practices, and relational networks.

113

We often think about the congregational life in terms of durability: Can we build something that will last? Is it sustainable with an economic model? These are the wrong questions. Can we help form disciples who will multiply? This is the true question. The church flourished for two thousand years not by staying the same but by finding unique enculturation in every people, culture, and place across the world. This will be true in the globalized network society as well. The uniqueness of these innovative faith communities will be as diverse as the people who cultivate them. As they proliferate across the cyberscape, the possibility of redeeming the technosphere may be in reach.

Three Stories

Both churches led by the authors launched multiple fresh expressions throughout the pandemic. These ranged across analog, digital, and hybrid settings. For example, Living Room Church is a network of Christians meeting digitally through Facebook Live and YouTube from their homes to pray, worship, have communion, and share in sermonic conversations. Yoga Church Digital transitioned from meeting in a studio to a live devotional and yoga practice broadcasted into people's homes over a streaming service called Streamyard. Supper Table Church was formed by young parents who found themselves isolated in quarantine when suddenly they became homeschool teachers overnight. We prepared themed meals, placed a screen at the supper table, and joined together digitally to eat, converse, pray, and share ideas. Paws of Praise Digital was a community of animal lovers who gathered with their pets on screens using Zoom rooms to share in conversations and showcase their pets' unique personalities.

Roz's church pivoted with one of its significant outreaches, English as a Second Language (ESL). It was hard enough in person to welcome any of their friends from other countries. After taking a pause immediately after COVID-19, they resumed in a more personal online format. They helped provide any technological needs for families, and the dedicated instructors ventured to do something that many public-school teachers have been doing: teach online. The smaller groups allowed students and teachers to go deeper in learning and to form meaningful friendships.

So, let's dig into three of these stories and how they evolved during the pandemic.

Analog to Digital

Yoga Church Digital—Pivoting to Online

Karen Hughes is the pioneer of Yoga Church Digital. She tells her story in the Livestream below, including some of the fresh expressions she has cultivated. Because of her ability to connect with people who are not-yet-Christians, and because of her years of experience as a personal trainer and certified yoga instructor, she is the qualified pioneer for yoga church.

Listen:

When COVID-19 began to spread, many people in Florida decided to shelter in place. It was no longer safe to gather people in-person for the yoga practice. The practice was life-giving to many participants and was a way to relieve anxiety and depression. The inability to gather was devastating for some. Karen was listening to the context; she saw that the virus, job losses, and social-political upheaval were causing people's anxiety to spike to new levels. This was broadcast on the daily news, blasted across people's social media feeds, as well as articulated through personal conversations.

Love:

Because Karen loves people deeply, she saw that what she could offer through yoga could bring healing and minimize the heightened anxiety. She saw the need and how her own mixture of personal skills and calling could make a difference. She was willing to sacrificially give her time and services (for which she was usually paid in a gym setting) to the netizens of cyberspace for free. She found a friend who had a bit of technological

115

know-how and launched the first session of Yoga Church Digital. Her team emailed participants from the earlier analog version of the group to let them know they would offer the gathering online. They gave some basic instructions: find a peaceful place, have a yoga mat ready, and perhaps light some candles. Then they just got started.

Community:

Karen's team created a Facebook event for the gatherings and posted it on numerous platforms. Some of the people who participated in analog Yoga Church invited their friends. Along with reaching out through emails and phone calls, the first group was invited to gather together on a Friday at 9:00 a.m. To open, people are given an opportunity to type their name, where they are from, and how they are feeling. An open invitation to people of "all faiths" or of "no faith" was given, as well as an alert that the gathering would be following the spiritual pathway of Jesus of Nazareth. Being a Christian is not required! A brief devotional from the Christian scriptures is offered, followed by the guided yoga practice, then concluded with prayer.

Share Jesus:

Hundreds of viewers began to join Digital Yoga Church each week from around the country. Many of these were people who would never come to the in-person version of the gathering. Friends invited more friends, shared the links, and through word of mouth told others. Participants were invited to post pictures and selfies from their makeshift yoga studios at home. This rippled out across the digital pond and more and more people started to become regulars. They began to check in every week with how meaningful the gathering was. Over time they began sharing prayers, requests, and concerns. People asked where they could make donations.

Karen perceived that community was really starting to form, so her team decided to have "Conversations for a Difference" after the gathering by Zoom. The conversation was advertised several weeks in advance. Participants were invited to come share about spiritual practices they were finding to be helpful during the quarantine. In the first gathering, several people shared how their faith in Jesus was really making a difference. One expressed their hang ups with the church and how she found her spiritual connection with mother earth. People across the spectrum spiritually were invited to keep coming and having the monthly conversation. Some are coming to faith, some are growing in their existing faith, and others remain aloof to faith, but they keep coming for the conversations.

Church:

For some practitioners of Yoga Church Digital, this is their *only* church. Each week they reflect on the devotional and integrate this into the intention of their yoga practice. They are learning to pray for the first time and exploring what faith in Jesus looks like. For others, this is an additional component of their Christian faith, and they participate in other church gatherings. And some come for the spiritual practice of yoga but remain closed to the Christian faith. This mixed community has become "church" in the same way that a Sunday morning worship service would be for longtime believers.

Repeat:

During the course of creating Yoga Church Digital (YCD), Karen has been busy planting other fresh expressions with her team. She has harnessed the learnings from this gathering and applied to other needs in the community. The idea inspired other pioneers to start their own fresh expressions using similar themes and technology. Some participants of YCD are planning how they can create their own version of the gathering themselves.

Supper-Table Church (a Digital Church)

Listen:

Many fresh expressions are born from the needs of those who plant them. Contextually intelligent pioneers know if they are experiencing some

117

need, then likely there are others. The Supper Table Church (STC) team consisted of parents with school-age children. When the pandemic erupted, they were stuck at home, isolated, with the kids in the house 24/7. This was a common theme across their social media accounts and inner circles.

Love:

The quarantine caused strained relationships in itself, but the added stress of trying to suddenly be homeschool teachers was an additional challenge. Not only did the parents feel clueless about homeschooling, they were also separated from any interaction with other adults. So, the team decided to invite other parents to a Zoom conversation. They listened to the needs the parents were expressing and shared the inability to get together over a meal. The idea for STC was really based on their own needs. They set a time, created social media events, and made a Zoom link available to all who wanted to join. They started to gather simply to love other parents struggling with isolation.

Community:

The parents invited other parents they knew who might want to join in. Suddenly people from Kentucky, Georgia, and Pennsylvania started participating. They propped a screen up at one empty seat at the table, prepared a meal, and sat down to chat. Someone asked if it would be okay to pray over the food. They swapped ideas about what was working and not working as homeschool parents. Each family shared what they cooked for the night and swapped recipes. Over time they decided to all cook a meal within the same theme: Italian, tacos, breakfast, and so on.

Share Jesus:

After meeting over these themed meals for several weeks, the parents were longing for something more than small talk and sharing struggles. One of the leaders on the team asked if it would be okay to share a "Jesus story" the following week. This would be a simple story from the life of Jesus, followed by a series of questions. All the families could agree that Jesus was a great teacher and that this would add a spiritual dimension to their time. People simply shared their thoughts around the question: "If this story happened today, what would it look like?" There were no right or wrong answers, only people's reflections. Occasionally, they would gather with the question: "If this story about Jesus is true, how could it make a difference in my life?"

Church:

Some of the families stopped attending for various reasons unique to their own family situations. A core group from STC formed deep and penetrating relationships. They began to text and call each other outside the group. Some broke off just to Zoom together and explore probing questions about their walks with Christ. The more mature believers began to serve as mentors to newbies in the faith. Some even started to read portions of the Bible in sync with each other and leave voice reflections on their impressions. They also began to have a time of Holy Communion during STC, in which they take the bread and drink portion of each meal to recall the life, death, resurrection of Jesus, and how he was present and fully alive in their midst.

Repeat:

Some people broke off the group to start a more local version with the friends in their neighborhood. Others were inspired to start similar groups with friends around other interests and concerns. The core team of STC decided that they could partner their churches together to offer hot meals to the community and then invite them to join their Zoom. The group has multiplied in several ways.

Drive-Thru Community Dinner Church (A Hybrid Story of St. Mark's UMC, Ocala, Florida)

Listen:

In the middle of the pandemic, Jill and I (Michael) were appointed additionally to St. Mark's UMC in Ocala, Florida. This was a struggling church in significant decline for over a decade. They were on the verge of closure due to decline in membership and finances. For many weeks the offering at St. Mark's was zero and worship attendees dropped below thirty. It is also a congregation near and dear to our hearts. This is the congregation where I was baptized, confirmed, came to faith, got sober, preached my first sermon, and where we were married and our children were baptized. The pandemic limited any of our old strategies from previous congregations.

We started Digital Home Visits with the long-term members through Zoom, listening to their stories. We formed a team to start "prayer walking" in the surrounding neighborhood. I appropriated a mass email list from my friend who was a community organizer. I sent an email out to over six hundred clergy, leaders, and help agencies. I simply let people know I was new to the community and would love to learn from what they were doing to serve the community. Three people responded, showing interest in having further conversation.

The month before we arrived, I utilized the "looking for recommendations" feature on Facebook, asking "What are the greatest needs and challenges in the Ocala community?" People began to respond with things like "racism" "food insecurity," "COVID-19," "police brutality," and so on. I responded to each person's thoughts, then invited the interested responders to help me facilitate a "Community Listening Session." We wanted to hear from the residents about their problems and challenges and how we might work together to fill the gaps between need and resources.

Next we created posters and in addition to "prayer walking" in the neighborhood, we knocked on doors inviting people to the listening session. When we held the listening session, we threw up all the greatest challenges and needs that people had on a white board and had conversation about which ones we thought had the most potential impact. It was discouraging that only twelve people showed up from the surrounding neighborhood. However, one of those twelve was Mrs. Betti Jefferson!

Love:

Betti was a "person of peace" in the community. She had been ministering to some of the populations experiencing poverty at the deepest levels. As we explored the greatest challenges, poverty and food insecurity were the most prominent recurring themes. Betti was facilitating semi-truck loads full of food being dropped in a vacant parking lot. She used social media and word of mouth to alert the community of the "food drops." Hundreds of people were showing up every week. "What I really need is space, and some refrigerators to store the food," Mrs. Betti said. Well, we just happen to have both! We combined with Betti, moving in some new refrigerators and gave her some dedicated space for her drops. We also decided that we would provide hot meals along with passing out the groceries for the week. Our church had a drive-thru portico area where people could pull up in their vehicles and we could serve them where they were.

Community:

We started the drive-thru community dinners with our skeleton crew of faithful servants, a kitchen crew preparing the meals, a delivery team, a prayer station team, an arts and crafts team for kids, and a group of us who would be floaters, holding up signs on the street corner and connecting with people as they came through. Our first gathering of over one hundred people came through! We found people were very open to conversation and shared about their struggles and fears. Many received prayer. But also, we started to have deep conversations as they waited for their meals. A recurring question arose: "When will this church open back up for worship?" We tried to explain that we were open for worship, but it was currently all online. We discovered that very few people would join in through the Zoom link we provided with their meals. We decided for this community that we would need to offer a safe, socially distanced, physical gathering.

Share Jesus:

In response to the community we were forming with those who came every week, we started the "Open Air Worship" under the same portico where they came to pick up their meals. This was a simple worship experience where we handed out a liturgy for people to follow. We prayed

121

together, shared joys and concerns, and had a short simple sermon. All this seemed to work quite well for this community. Friends from drive-thru community dinners; recovery fellowships; and Open Arms Village, a center for men experiencing homelessness housed on our property, began to resonate with the gatherings. A little church plant alongside the existing church has begun to form.

Church:

For many, Drive-Thru Community Dinners is their "church." They look forward to the brief time of connection, prayer, and a hot meal. And Open Air Worship has become a safe place to land for many who encounter us for the first time through a hot meal in the middle of a pandemic. We keep checking in with them, asking what worship should look like and if they would like to contribute week after week. Alongside Betti Jefferson and her amazing leadership in the community, this little church has begun to form and grow. Some of the attendees make a journey back to the inherited congregation, some in the inherited congregation have made their way into this new church springing up from the neighborhood, and others call this space alone their church home. All of this is good, and the connections have so much potential.

Repeat:

The drive-thru dinner and open-air worship have not been around long enough to multiply. The pattern of multiplication is inherent in the growth of the groups itself. A distinct faith-community, catalyzed by Facebook and neighborhood connections, moved from simple drive-thru meals to a new Christian community in its own right. Churches from around the area are coming to learn from what we are doing. This tiny church on the edge of death is feeding hundreds of people every week. We don't know if the inherited church will survive this challenging season, but the multiplication lies in all those who are coming to faith, or coming back to faith, through a handful of believers listening to their community. This continues to be a hybrid of digital and analog church, as it is what's contextually appropriate for this community.

App It

Chat Box

Gather with your team physically or digitally and discuss the following questions.

1. Do I have a team to start this new expression (at least one other person willing to start something new with me)?

2. Do we have a "person of peace" (Luke 10:6) in this community, practice, hobby, organization, space, or affinity group?

3. How are we listening to God and the people in this analog or digital space? (For example, we will pray for the people in a particular social-media stream every day for ten minutes; we will observe the needs people describe on a particular page, group, website, or chat; we will host a listening session for people to articulate the greatest challenges they are facing; we will spend time in a first, second, third place simply making prayerful observations, etc.)

4. What group of people is God leading us to in particular?

5. How are we identifying their needs?

6. Do we have any "digital real estate," a space where people can gather?

7. Are we looking to cultivate a community that is:

   (a) digital: this group will start and remain primarily digital in nature;

   (b) analog: this group will be primarily analog in nature, but we will use digital means to connect people; or

   (c) hybrid: this group will be a mixture of digital and analog?

E-haviors

Consider how these practices might be helpful as missionaries in the digital age.

1. **Spend time doing tasks that require sustained attention:** Math, reading, art, or deep conversation. These counteract the damage that technology can do to the brain.

2. **Meditation:** This is even more important than ever in the digital age to rest the hyper-stimulated brain. Plan daily times to break away to still the mind.

3. **Turn off useless apps:** Most of the apps on your phone are unnecessary. Know the ones that really work for you and discard the ones you don't need.

4. **Turn off all notifications:** Your phone, watch, or tablet have a job to do . . . to attract you to look at them! One way this is accomplished is through notifications. Every time someone likes a post, retweets, or texts, this will draw you to the device, which causes disconnection of presence in whatever you are doing. We have discovered that notifications are completely unnecessary. You can review all that's happened in your scheduled online times.

5. **Don't send or respond to annoying personal messages!:** We've all been on the receiving end of the "pass this on," "keep this going," "watch this and share!," or "if you want to be blessed . . ." Don't do it, ever! It's the most annoying thing in the digital world. Never respond to them, and don't even give people the satisfaction of opening them.

6. **Get off the screen and have an in-person conversation:** There have been days when we stayed in Zoom rooms from morning till night. We've all felt the fatigue of digital engagement. What counters this is face-to-face, molecule-swapping conversations with friends and loved ones. We need to seek a good balance between the two.

Livestream: Karen Hughes

I am Karen Lambert Hughes. I am a layperson and Fresh Expressions pioneer. I have been in love with Jesus from the time I was a little girl praying for children who are hungry or sick, praying for those who are not loved or are in need. I think I learned from a young age forgiveness, compassion for others, and a deep desire to help those in need. In my life journey Jesus has brought me through many trials.

As I became a middle-aged adult, it was easy for me to understand this new kind of church called Fresh Expressions. I am always trying different fresh expressions. I started first by being transparent with the people I hang out with in my own life—for example, my running club, swim club, and classes that I teach like boot camp and yoga. I have promoted and planted neighborhood dinner churches.

When COVID-19 changed our world, it was easy to do what I love in a different way—digitally. Actually, I am not very technologically savvy; however, with the help of those who are it was a go. With Yoga Church the context is for those wanting peace of mind, body, and spirit.

Yoga Church Digital (YCD) was formed using Facebook and You-Tube Live. We can be inclusive inviting all faiths, all believers or unbelievers with Rev. Michael Beck leading a devotion that plants the seed of Christ. Michael is great at applying the devotional application to life as it is today. The invitation is there to contemplate this message for our own lives during the yoga practice. In doing this we have an opportunity to create an intention to reflect or meditate on in order to strengthen the mind, body, and Spirit, creating restoration and healing through the renewal of our spirit. Our worship is in bodily movement with a Christ-centered intention. YCD is a great way to build community, listen through comments online, explore discipleship, pray for one another, and be church for those without a church.

We have found other ways to reach those with the love of Jesus. We have a Drive-Thru Dinner Church once a week that continues to grow; with this fresh expression we are serving families who are hungry—physically and spiritually. We are able to show them the love of Jesus as they drive up to receive a delicious dinner with homemade desserts, garlic bread, and salad (made by parishioners wanting to give back). We offer Jesus-themed crafts for children and a Zoom link that will give the drive-thru participants the opportunity to go home and link into a Jesus story. Finally, what is really awesome is that most people pull their vehicle over and pray with us.

We also do a pancake breakfast called Connect (a Messy Church meeting in the MLK Jr. Center). It is more of a walk-thru as most don't have vehicles in this neighborhood. It is run with the same idea as the Drive-Thru Dinner Church. Before COVID-19, for ten to twelve months we had built up this fresh expression, serving pancakes, sausage, and juice. It took a while to build the trust of the neighborhood, as we were very different in many ways. We did end up building a community breakfast where we had lots of fun, worshipped through Jesus stories, played children's games, and had conversation and prayer. Connect is a growing community of serving, listening, worshipping, loving, and being church.

We need to be the hands, feet, and voice of Jesus in this changing world, and it can be done digitally. In fact, we are reaching more people with the use of digital means now than ever before.

Going Old-School in a New-School World

Meeting "relational needs" by building circles of connection through delivering care packages, snail-mail, and other meaningful deliverables to show appreciation.

COVID-19 was a catalyst for what was already in process: a technological and digital economy advancing for good as well as for harm in every sector of society. We live in a technocracy that bestows many blessings upon its citizens, yet it comes with a price: *we find ourselves in another Great Depression.* Americans have been suffering with depression, loneliness, and anxiety for many years. A report from The American Psychiatric Association indicated that from 2016 to 2017 "the proportion of adults who described themselves as more anxious than the previous year was at 36 percent."[1] These statistics not only pertain to adults but also affect young adolescents. For example, "a 2017 study of over half a million 8th through 12th graders found that the number exhibiting high levels of depressive symptoms increased by 33 percent between 2010 and 2015. In the same period, the suicide rate for girls in that age group increased by 65 percent."[2] For adults and adolescents, a link exists between the usage or overconsumption of social media and the incidence of loneliness and depression.[3] So, is social media really social? It depends on how much or why a person relies on it.

When conceiving fresh expressions in a digital age, this link means that while we can leverage technology to further the gospel, other methods and practices of engagement should be rediscovered. It means going old-school in a new world to show God's love and radical hospitality.

During COVID-19, many churches struggled to keep in touch with people in their congregations through means other than digital formats—and sadly, many people were displaced in the shuffle. Many suffered loneliness, isolation, and depression while neglecting their spiritual lives and exercises to nurture their whole being. Whether this is an individual problem or a collective problem, it's clear that church leaders need to reconceive its current measures for keeping its people in the loop. The online platform is either not enough for some individuals or they have grown tired of it, and some have become unchurched in the process. Anecdotally, some pastors are estimating that 20 percent of participants have given up their relationships with their congregation. We wish this were not the case, and we all know that it happens regardless of pandemic or other cultural shifts.

A classic marketing slogan comes to mind. Roz remembers in the 1980s the viral AT&T slogan that took on a life of its own: "reach out and touch someone." The slogan encouraged people to pick up their telephone (AT&T had a monopoly) to reach out to friends and family. As kids, we would say "reach out and touch someone" and playfully smack or punch each other. However, this slogan took on new meaning for me when I was in the Marine Corps. As we went on ten, twenty, thirty, or forty-mile hikes with our packs, getting tired out was guaranteed. To ensure nobody fell behind, the sergeant or senior enlisted Marine, who called cadence, would occasionally appropriate that familiar slogan, "reach out and touch someone." Once that command was called, you were expected to touch the Marine's back in front of you—if you didn't keep up, the whole unit would slow down and recalibrate. The central point of this exercise was not to allow anyone to fall behind the pack.

During a time of physical distancing, many people consequently became *socially* distant. We have retreated from once familiar places that we would often frequent, all to ensure the safety of ourselves and those around us. The distance caused many to be isolated, lonely, and depressed. A vaccine does not cure this side-effect. We have become distant from others and perhaps God. According to a recent Barna Study in 2020, daily scripture engagement had already been declining but worsened during the pandemic: "In January, 27.8 percent of American adults were Bible engaged. By June, after months of quarantine and church closures, that figure was down to 22.6 percent."[4] The downward slope took place in the height of the COVID-19 pandemic when people had more free time than usual, were working from home, and could for the most part set their own schedules.

Relational touches are vital and should stretch beyond the digital world. Although the problem appears to be simply described, the effort requires time, energy, and the help of a team. To be effective, it moves wider than the pastor or pioneer and church staff. This is an opportunity to develop a circle of care with laity and others who have the passion for involvement in congregational care. The struggle for those that operate more in the apostolic, prophetic, or evangelistic (APE) efforts is the lack of affinity for pastoral care.[5] It doesn't mean a spiritual entrepreneur can't operate in shepherding and pastoral gifts, but these behaviors may need the muscles that are not worked as often. It is similar to the person in the gym who only works their upper body but neglects their leg muscles. Doing lifts like squats can actually help increase strength to the upper body: "65 percent of your muscle is below your belt. It's your legs, your thighs, your glutes, your calves, and your hamstrings."[6] In the same vein, pastoral care represents the leg muscles in the local church. Leaders and followers understand the theological reasons for pastoral care (love your neighbor). However, this practice requires intentional introduction among new faith communities and fresh expression, to live into Isaiah 61:1-3:

> The LORD God's spirit is upon me,
> because the LORD has anointed me.
> He has sent me to bring good news to the poor,
> to bind up the brokenhearted,
> to proclaim release for captives,
> and liberation for prisoners,

to proclaim the year of the LORD's favor
and a day of vindication for our God,
to comfort all who mourn,
to provide for Zion's mourners,
to give them a crown in place of ashes,
oil of joy in place of mourning,
a mantle of praise in place of discouragement.
They will be called Oaks of Righteousness,
planted by the LORD to glorify himself.

When reaching out to those who need a personalized touch, your context will determine your methodology. However, here are some suggestions that can become catalysts for application.

Most churches and individuals have access to a database from which they retrieve phone numbers and addresses. Systems are important. Most pioneers and church planters we know are gifted on the relational side but have difficulty implementing internal systems, which is precisely why you need other people to complement your gifts.

To make a larger impact, you have to get smaller. These practices aren't meant particularly for a pandemic because in the future after the crisis subsides, relational touches will become more important as larger group gatherings find new equilibrium in a post-COVID-19 world. Many churches and leaders during the pandemic learned to maximize every phone number in their database. Everyone on their list receives periodic phone calls. The list is split up between unpaid servants and folks who are passionate about care. It didn't cost extra in data charges, only time and discipline. And while we are aware that time is something we will never get back, making those types of calls is something you won't regret. You should utilize a team to do it, we can't stress that enough. And a word of caution: don't annoy people or bug them. Call them once every three months or so, at a sensible rate that won't interfere with people's busy lives—and have each person making the calls take any significant notes. Share it on Google Drive for everyone involved in the aspect of care to see who has been called, or what any particular prayer request was, and ask if they know how to access the worship services. Roz's general practice around the calls has been to keep them short and ask those two major questions. If the opportunity presents itself, you can pray with them on the phone. From experience, 99 percent of people will be grateful someone from a given faith community took the time to call and check up on them. Care teams can then gather virtually to debrief and discuss anything they learned, including parishioners' needs and the next steps in moving the team forward. Care teams are a service opportunity for folks who have plenty of free time, find themselves retired, or are seeking a way to give back that won't require them to leave the house.

Another relatively easy way to go old-school is to start a card-writing initiative. People are no longer used to receiving hand-written personalized mail. However, like phone calls, a majority of people are appreciative of a handwritten card. Hand-written notes and cards add some soul to a message that is lost in a digital format such as emails. The cost is low in terms of cards and stamps, but the return is high.

During lockdown, Roz had both toddlers at home with him and his wife, Callie. They both work full-time in various roles and are still trying to have creative and engaging days with their girls. Roz incorporated both his girls in the card-writing relationships. Roz wasn't trying to get his daughters to do his work. Rather he allowed them to color in their own way on each of the cards that went out. And then he simply added a line about how his daughters wanted to make people feel special with their work of art.

If you are able to capture people's birthday into the contact database, you can do something as simple as write birthday cards. This simple engagement is the essence of pastoral care. As the old adage goes: *It's the thought that counts.* Again, it's important to have a team in place, so that the workload doesn't fall on any one person. Anyone can do card writing. A team of people with a bit of extra time can easily be assembled and can write a few cards a week. Roz's team made sure everyone in their faith community received at least one card during lockdown. It was a small gesture that went a long way for people to feel cared for and engaged by the church. The phone calls and the card writing became a regular rhythm even outside of quarantine and will continue to be an important step of going old-school in a post-COVID-19 world.

Another idea, which is a bit pricier but definitely worth the return, is to send a small gift to individuals. Roz's team decided to send out small palm-branch crosses for Palm Sunday with an invitation to participate in online worship. Roz's team tested it first to see if it would go through the mail and if there were any hiccups to note. The palm-branch crosses looked good and had not been damaged in transit, so they decided to move forward. Again, the response was incredible because it brought familiarity to people who were used to receiving palm branches on Palm Sunday. The team made sure everyone had it before Palm Sunday, and many parishioners took pictures of the crosses and posted them on social media because they were blown away by the small gesture. If your budget allows for it, what would it look like to target a few special times in the year around holidays to make these kinds of efforts? What would work in your context that would be meaningful for folks in your faith community?

Phone calls and mailings are only two suggestions. But care packages can also be a gesture that creates meaningful moments for both the individuals doing the delivery and for the recipient. This can include delivering cookies, snack bags, children's activity packs, meals, and hermetically sealed communion elements to people's homes. You don't need to knock on the door and go inside the home; simply leave a note and the gift on the doorstep. These efforts are more time consuming but are still a way to create a personal touch. Also, it is a great way to involve children and students in the preparation and delivery process. Roz witnessed first-hand how the parents of four students participated and organized the care efforts to impact many. This not only teaches skills of time-management and teamwork but encourages children to foster their natural caring instincts. Service doesn't have to be segmented for specific age groups, but families can participate in the mission of the church together.

Another way to meet the pastoral needs of your faith community is by creating a safe and easy touchpoint through events like drive-thru prayer and communion. Many churches have practiced these methods and were able to encounter not only people in their churches but also the wider community. One of those churches was the Gospel Alliance Church in Belle Vernon, Pennsylvania. People pulled up under the church portico in their cars; sometimes it was individuals, other times whole families with children. People didn't even have to leave their cars. When the vehicle pulled up, the two-person prayer team was able to engage them in a meaningful conversation and a time of prayer. Two simple questions opened the door for interaction:

- What would you like Jesus to do for you today?
- How can we pray for you?

These moments did not include a sermon, handouts, or any other elements of worship. The motive was simple, and as one parishioner put it: "If they're feeling lonely, disconnected or overwhelmed, we want to offer a safe place for them to receive prayer."[7] The mission was accomplished. It didn't cost money, need approval by a committee, or necessarily require a pastor or paid church staff. Lay leaders can take on the opportunity and rise to the occasion.

Drive-thru communion can also be a meaningful way to create the same type of warmth and connection. Pastor Choi of Minden United Methodist Church was excited about the opportunity, and it was not difficult to pull off. Social distancing was observed, and the hermetically sealed individual elements were given through car windows by people wearing gloves and masks.[8] These practices are not only something that can be done during a global pandemic but are a way to build ongoing interaction in a post-COVID-19 world.

Going old-school applies not only to meeting the care needs in your faith community but also in your surrounding community. Several other faith communities organize drive-by parades and drive-thru prayer trains to show love to first responders, hospitals, patients, nursing home staff, and residents. Of course, this means obtaining permission because a church doesn't want to interrupt the important functions of these entities. After the permissions are obtained, the gesture is an easy one and only takes coordination. As spiritual entrepreneurs, in the past these opportunities fostered partnerships by providing meals, drinks, and other gifts of love to first responders and law enforcement. In the height of COVID-19, churches stepped in to show appreciation for the unsung heroes in our society along with those who were "essential" workers who had no option of staying home. Of course, there are times when churches and Christ-followers get it wrong—but there are times we get it right, and during the height of a global pandemic churches leveraged their financial and people resources to make an impact. It is participating in mission with God. As one missiologist put it, "The Church doesn't have a mission, but the mission has a Church."[9] The theological concept of the *mission dei* means being sent out by a sending God. When the church lives as sent one, we are sent out into all the world meeting needs in our own faith communities and all those we can reach with God's love. Christians are not invoking God's presence on people and places but finding the ways in which God is already at work and knowing that God's prevenient grace was already at work in the hearts and lives of people before any one Christian or church arrived on the scene.

Old-school caregiving is incarnational ministry that Jesus lived out and practiced in his ministry. Eugene Peterson's paraphrase in *The Message: The Bible in Contemporary Language*, perceives this incarnation in the poetry of John 1:1:

> The Word became flesh and blood,
>   and moved into the neighborhood.
> We saw the glory with our own eyes,
>   the one-of-a-kind glory,
>   like Father, like Son,
> Generous inside and out,
>   true from start to finish.[10]

Jesus was present among his disciples and was/is "God with skin on" for the people Jesus interacted with on a daily basis. Though ministry has varied and changed since then, the message remains the same, even if the wineskins change. The temptation is to go with what is trendy, easy, and offers the highest return with the lowest effort. Personal touches require work and time. Yes, it can be draining and exhausting if you are an introvert; or—given a crisis—even if you are an extrovert; or if you rely on shepherding and pastoral gifts. However, as much as ministry wineskins change, something that will never go out of style and will still bear fruit is the personal, incarnational approach to ministry. Find out what is contextual for your setting. Don't rely so much on the digital format that you forsake the personal, and don't overemphasize the personal without using what Roz calls the "air attack." It takes both boots on the ground and an air attack to reach a diverse community, both within your local congregation and outside of it.

App It

Chat Box

Gather with your team physically or digitally and discuss the following questions.

1. What are some creative ways you've "gone old-school in a new-school world?"

2. How are you striking a balance between digital connection and in-person engagements?

3. Is anyone in your church open to a "care package" ministry, or sending handwritten notes or cards?

4. Are the leaders of your church organized to "watch over one another in love"? Who is doing most of the pastoral care in your congregation? How might you distribute that through teams?

5. How have you helped the most isolated in your church know they are loved and cared for?

6. Who heads up that area of ministry? Might there be someone among you particularly called to this work?

E-haviors

Consider how these practices might be helpful as missionaries in the digital age.

1. **Creating habitats of listening in the digital ecosystem**: Use social media to ask questions, find out what peoples' needs are, and

what is good news to them. Rather than making witty statements to attract interaction, ask compelling questions that provoke people to share.

2. **Protecting the connection (frequency of meeting with your team):** Social distancing, or being separated physically, strains relationships. Find ways to get together often. If you are limited by restrictions for meeting in-person, meet frequently in a digital platform. Sustaining relationships is harder in this venue.

3. **Re-present Christ in cyberscape:** Think about how a post, tweet, picture, or video will represent Christ? When posting things be aware of your motivations. On digital platforms you are never off the clock when it comes to representing Jesus.

4. **Creating community pages:** Every fresh expression needs to have some digital real estate. You can create free pages, groups, and events on Facebook for instance. This is a prime opportunity to collect like-minded friends around a cause or idea. Have your team invite their friends, whom you may not know, to events and pages.

5. **Tagging:** This is simply the practice of adding words, phrases, or names to digital content. This marks the content to identify it as belonging to a particular category or concerning a particular person or topic. Hashtags help connect your content to a larger audience. Tagging friends who participate in digital communities alerts friends in their larger network that they are involved.

6. **Remixing:** Some of the newest technologies, films, music, and trends are remixes of older versions. Rather than disposing of things, remix them. You can even take older content and reuse it in new ways. For instance, doing a "watch party" of an older worship experience, adding video clips to existing worship experiences to remake them, and so on.

7. **Archiving:** Make sure you strategically store digital content and ideas. Always have backup files for important things. You can share your resources through cloud-based technologies as well. Offer what you create for free for others to use.

8. **Rating:** Be generous and kind in your classification or ranking of someone or something based on a comparative assessment of his, her, or its quality, standard, or performance. Christians have a

reputation of being stingy and critical. This is a counter-cultural mark of being a Christian in digital space. Rating is how people decide they will try something or not. Don't be dishonest, but remember what Jesus said: "rate onto others as you would have them rate unto you"—or something like that!

Livestream:
Olu Brown

I'm Olu Brown. In March 2020, I was on the road speaking at a seminary in Philadelphia when the COVID-19 reality unfolded with public health mandates. I immediately shifted to my multi-tasking zone and upheld my commitment to speak *and* keep in touch with our worship and administrative teams at Impact Church in Atlanta, Georgia. In fewer than forty-eight hours, like many other churches, we made a decision to host all adult in-person experiences online and discontinue our in-person children's and youth experiences until further notice.

Our worship team shifted from live worship experiences on the stage in our church to pre-recorded worship sets in the home of the music director. Our preaching team shifted from proclaiming the Word of God in person to pre-recording sermons outside or in our homes. What we thought was normal and would last forever suddenly changed, and the church had been disrupted all over the world. There was no going back, only forward.

The two most important decisions during the pandemic were to gather the church and communicate digitally:

First, recall John 4:23: "But the time is coming—and is here!—when true worshippers will worship in spirit and truth." The church was never about brick and mortar and we needed to encourage our team and congregation that meeting in a church building for worship, small groups, or any other type of gathering didn't guarantee God's presence, and that the original plan for the church was to become a community not bound by walls. The church of Jesus Christ is wherever the spirit of the Lord is. That is good news because the spirit of the Lord is everywhere. Helping people break out of the routine of being in a building wasn't easy, but it was necessary and it helped us continue to reach people for Christ.

Second, we recommitted to a dual platform of communication that embraced in-person and virtual methods. We always utilized both platforms for worship, but we needed to extend this philosophy into every event and program for the foreseeable future. From the first stages of the pandemic, our team members began planning programs formatted for both in-person and virtual viewership to ensure all people could be connected to the life and ministry of the church. Ministry team members had to think differently about planning ministry. For example, as we plan Vacation Bible School, the planning process must begin with an in-person and virtual experience format.

We realized the world would never be the same again, and that meant the church had to change in fulfillment of Matthew 28:19: "Therefore, go and make disciples of all nations." For years to come, this gospel mandate will respond to health and wellbeing mandates in an unstable world. The key to discipleship and reaching people for Christ in our new normal is to be flexible and to always prepare worship, programs, and events for dual platforms, both in-person and virtual.

From Monologues to Dialogues

One major gift the pandemic provided was an opportunity to rethink the preparation and delivery of sermons. In Protestant churches the sermon is a central component of the worship service. Over half of a one-hour service is dedicated to the reading of the scripture, proclamation of the sermon, and an opportunity for hearers to respond in some way.

In the digital space, even the most gifted orators across the country noticed that viewership was decreasing during the sermon time. Eventually, following the initial stages of the pandemic and the newfound interest in church services now streaming live all over the internet, viewership decreased across the board. Even long-term church members began to grow apathetic toward online worship and became critical, particularly of the sermon. Why?

Recall McLuhan's prophetic wisdom that "the medium is the message." Because the effects of technology go deep, the medium shapes our patterns of sensation and perception. Unfortunately, screens and monitors orient our minds toward "the shallows." As Nicholas Carr writes: "What both enthusiast and skeptic miss is what McLuhan saw: that in the long run a medium's content matters less than the medium itself in influencing how we think and act. As our window onto the world, and onto ourselves, a popular medium molds what we see and how we see it—and eventually, if we use it enough, it changes who we are, as individuals and as a society."[1]

Unfortunately one of the side effects of long-term engagement with electronic media is a diminished capacity for long-term sustained attention.

Preachers are familiar with a well-known saying, "the mind can only take what the butt can stand." We can rephrase this for the online culture, "the mind can only receive what can be stimulated through the screen." In the digital medium, we need to think about the people on the other side of the screen and their experience. An unfortunate gut-check for preachers like us who love to deliver thirty-minute riveting sermons that jar the hearers at every turn, is that most observers were checking out from the sermon a few minutes into the presentation, even in a sanctuary space.

In the pandemic, when we all had to figure out how to do "online church," there was a sharp learning curve. Many clergy discovered they had to learn an entirely new skill set, moving from well-polished, staged, propositional monologues to facilitating dialogical conversations. Emerging generations have been disconnected from the idea of being "preached to" for decades. Yet preachers accelerated this instinct to "preach to" in the face of COVID-19. Many pioneers discovered in the isolation of quarantine that people yearned to be heard and known. They began experimenting with ways to facilitate this through online worship.

In most fresh expressions of church, there's not a formal moment when the religious professional stands up to tell us what the Bible means and how to apply it personally. Rather, there's a conversation around a "Jesus story" or a few verses of biblical text.[2] Someone frames the text or story, provides a little background, and then asks open-ended, non-confrontational questions. In these nascent Christian communities, people situate across the spectrum in their faith journey, everything from not-yet-Christians, to no-longer Christians, to opposed-to-faith Christians, to committed followers of Christ. We can't assume people are working from any theological consensus in the group. One of the keys to engagement is crafting questions that don't have a "right or wrong" answer but to plug into the postmodern tendency to share from personal experience. That doesn't mean there's no right or wrong behaviors, but people should come to those realizations for themselves. Actually, the Bible itself does the heavy lifting, not our forceful oratorical flourish.

This leveling is amplified in the technosphere. As people scroll through their social media feeds and suddenly find themselves in our "worship experience," we have a very small window of opportunity to engage them in a way that connects. The robed professional standing in the empty sanctuary, delivering a theological treatise (usually written out on manuscript or teleprompter) is the wrong approach if evangelism is part of the purpose. It reinforces negative stereotypes people have (particularly from cable television) about the church.

By analogy, think of worship in a public digital forum as a means for experiencing a church service in the middle of the town square. People are passing through, traveling the flows of their everyday routines, and are usually just passing by. There is a small crowd of devoted followers there with us, and indeed we are ministering to, for, and with them, but we can't focus the service solely on them. Every worship experience in cyberspace is *both* for the people gathered with us on the square *and* for those just passing by.

In short, every worship experience in the digital medium is an evangelistic event with potential not-yet-Christians and an opportunity for spiritual formation of already-Christians. This means we take a hybrid approach in our online worship.

C. H. Dodd, in *The Apostolic Preaching and Its Developments,* explains the difference between preaching and teaching, maintaining that preaching "is the public proclamation of Christianity to the non-Christian world."[3] Preaching in a pre-Christian world primarily involved the *kerygma*, which was utterly centered in sharing the life, death, and resurrection of Jesus, and its significance. We need to recover the importance of this in a post-Christian world as well.

For many centuries, clergy have been "preaching to the choir," quite literally. We've heard colleagues jokingly say, "We need to start with getting people in the church saved first!" This is unfortunately true as well. However, the attractional church is largely a pastor-teacher centered model, in which training up the flock in the historic faith is the primary work. Primarily inherited church systems are seeking to nurture already-Christians in the life of faith. Those with more apostolic, prophetic, and evangelistic gift sets get pushed to the periphery.

However, when we are speaking into the sea of billions of netizens, we need to be careful what we are communicating. We know that all people are at different levels regarding what kind of spiritual food they can digest. As Paul writes, "I gave you milk to drink instead of solid food, because you weren't up to it yet" (1 Cor 3:2). Laying out a juicy steak (e.g., exploring the penal substitutionary theory of the atonement) is probably not the best approach in a digital medium. It may be a riveting experience for long-term Christians in certain traditions, but it will alienate many hearers who may be leaning in to explore the faith. The primitive preaching always ended with some version of invitation, an appeal to a new way of seeing the world, an offer of forgiveness, the outpouring of God's grace in the life of the hearer.[4] The primary assumption is that the Holy Spirit is working through the heart of the hearer, wooing, guiding, convicting, and embracing.

These essential ingredients can be reappropriated for the new missional frontier. Missional practitioners have discovered that presenting Jesus, and asking questions, seems to be the most appropriate way to catalyze this kind of reflection in the hearers.

Sermonic Conversations

So, let's rethink how we present the gospel in a post-Christian, networked society. In an emerging form of Christian community, the sermon is present, but it takes a different form. Some retooling is necessary for many seminary-trained ministers, who prepare carefully revised manuscripts to be delivered from a pulpit to an existing flock of already-Christians.

The art of sermonic conversation is not a new phenomenon. It was in fact the preferred method of Jesus's teaching. Jesus's favorite teaching approach was to ask questions.

In *Jesus, The Master Teacher* Herman Horne examines the pedagogy of Jesus. Particularly useful is the analysis of how Jesus won and kept the attention of his hearers. Horne describes two kinds of attention:

- Voluntary. With effort.
- Involuntary. Without the sense of effort. With interest.

Horne shows that Jesus received both kinds of attention, "His willing disciples attended involuntarily. His unwilling auditors and critics, hearing him, not because they wanted to obey but to entrap him in his talk, gave voluntary attention."[5]

Jesus secured attention first, according to Horne, because he was an interesting person doing interesting things, but secondly because he knew how to get people's attention. He called for it when he spoke the words, "Listen up," "Hear," "Pay attention," or "If you have ears to hear." Next he pre-announced his coming by sending ahead teams of disciples (Luke 10). He utilized posture, he stood, he sat, and so on. Jesus spoke in "concrete, pictorial, imaginative language, which easily catches and holds the attention, as a moving picture does today." And he used "the familiar to explain the unfamiliar" to name a few methods.[6] Horne writes:

> We may also say that Jesus received attention because he paid attention. He saw and was interested in what people were doing and saying, and in their needs, and in helpful sympathy he drew his soul out unto them. His works prepared the way for his words.[7]

Can we achieve what Horne calls a "point of contact" with people in the online ecosystem? Can we create spaces where we can "pay attention" to people using digital technologies created to monetize our own attention? Can we use the same algorithms and mechanisms that prompt us to consume instead to cherish people made in the image of God? Can we take a system that programs us for the shallows and use it against itself, to bring people into deeper relationships?

This is what we're trying to accomplish with our variations on Living Room Church. We envision people sitting in their home space disoriented by the pandemic and give them a platform to be seen and heard. Each week we bring special guests to share from their own experiences how they are growing spiritually in the midst of the chaos and uncertainty. Someone on the team would offer a sermonic "lead-in," in a teaching style and fewer than eighteen minutes, on the designated biblical passage. Then people were invited to reflect on what resonated with them.

The Power of Questions

Asking questions was the primary way that Jesus established a point of contact to engage the attention of his hearers. Martin Copenhaver reports that Jesus asked a total of 307 questions.[8] By using the New International Version translation, J. R. Briggs counted 297 direct questions in the Gospels (105 questions in Matthew, sixty-seven in Mark, 101 in Luke, and fifty-one in John), and an additional twenty-seven "indirect questions through characters and figures embedded in the parables, as a way to advance the plot of these stories."[9]

The twenty-seven "parabolic questions," says Briggs, Jesus used as rhetorical devices to keep the listeners' attention. He was creating points of contact for listeners to be heard, locating themselves in the parables. These story-based questions were an intimate connection to the hearers. One post-resurrection question in Acts 9:4 is directed at Saul on the road to Damascus: "Saul, Saul, why are you harassing me?" By combining the repeated questions in the parallel stories of the Synoptic Gospels, Briggs shows that Jesus asked a total of 236 unique questions.[10]

When we examine the teaching of Jesus in this way, we see where some approaches to preaching don't connect with people not yet in church. Most sermons are a biblical exegesis to help the congregation understand and respond to the guidance of scripture. This doesn't work well if it is a conversation between the text and the preacher. By opening the sermonic setting to questions, the exploration takes unexpected twists and turns. Even the most creative preachers are more skilled at presenting persuasive points or applications than in guiding a conversation. It's hard work to accommodate and guide the actual reflections people bring to the text.

Sermonic conversations, like a well-formed *lectio divina* class, can be deeply transformative for the community. We start with a biblical text, we engage that text together, we locate ourselves in the story or epistle or poetry, and finally wrestle with the implications for our lives.

Lessons from Steve Jobs

When we suddenly found ourselves digital missionaries due to CO-VID-19, we instinctively knew from Fresh Expressions start-ups that we would need to adapt our worship to the new context. We couldn't just transplant what we did before into a digital medium. The medium itself transforms the experience of worship for the participants.

I (Michael) quickly looked around for a mentor or guide on this crazy new journey. I found one in the late Steve Jobs. I began watching Steve's talks, all stored for free on YouTube. I started to observe how he used technology, how he presented himself, how he adapted his message for the hearers at each presentation. He was playing up to the thousands of people that gathered for new product releases, but his wider audience was those who would experience his talks through the entirely digital medium.

I read Carmine Gallo's book, *The Presentation Secrets of Steve Jobs: How to Be Insanely Great in Front of Any Audience.* Gallo lays out Jobs's approach in three acts: act one, create the story; act two, deliver the experience; act three, refine and rehearse. Nuggets are included in the description for how to use technology to bring hearers into a story.

Steve Jobs "shared the stage" in presentations. Jobs always featured supporting characters who performed key roles in the narrative.

For the church leader, this reminds us that evangelism, discipleship, preaching, and church planting are not each a solo act. Moves of the Spirit flow through the life of every participant, believer, and skeptic, as we live in community with others. In a digital culture with values like sharing, crowdsourcing, and remixing, enabled by free tech, we need to think of every gathering as a team event. This is even true of sermons. The best communicators help everyone involved "shine for the good of the show."[11]

In a digital medium the brain craves variety, at the risk of distraction. The brain won't stay engaged on anything that's boring. No single communicator can hold an audience's full attention for long periods of time, no matter how skilled. However, there are ways to introduce variety into a presentation that sustains the attention of the brain. Gallo shows that the best communicators in history typically stayed within a well-defined duration.

Great speech writers have practiced this for years. Speeches written for John F. Kennedy, Ronald Reagan, and Barack Obama were scripted to last no longer than twenty minutes. Of course, a Jobs keynote presentation lasted much longer—approximately one and a half hours—but Jobs kept it interesting by incorporating demonstrations, video clips, and—very importantly—guest speakers.[12]

The tactic of using "guest speakers" is very important for effective sermonic conversations. So, guess who the guests are? They are mostly or typically the people within the gathered community. Just as Jesus invited people into his teaching with questions, we can grab the attention of our hearers by inviting them into the conversation and really listening to what they are saying. Whether that is spoken out in digital space or typed in a chat.

In Living Room Church, we try to incorporate these things we have learned into the experience:

- we imitate the "Steve Jobs style" (story-based, simple, unscripted);

- we follow the TED Talk Rule for our sermonic lead (eighteen minutes maximum, which is a time frame tested in TED Talk research);

- we change the screen every three to five minutes;

- we are intentionally invitational (multiple engagement points to offer feedback or join in); and

- we leave space for "guest speakers" (anyone who wants to share their thoughts).

Additionally, we found that live, not pre-recorded, through multiple streams (StreamYard, Facebook, YouTube), with dialogue not monologue, and a team of digital ministers (engaging people, asking questions, and welcoming people throughout the experience) are also key to engagement.

Biggie Smalls famously said "more money more problems," but we think it's also true that "more mission more problems." As we find ways to creatively engage not-yet-Christians, it creates new problems we didn't anticipate. For instance, in a flattened conversation we struggle to manage the contributions of certain dominant personalities, while drawing out the profound wisdom of more quiet participants. We've learned that getting visitors' contact information and following up right away with digital "home visits" and "meet and greets" after gatherings is essential. Providing lots of "opt in" opportunities throughout the week is also important. Finally, in a "membership adverse" society we have had to redefine what "membership" actually means. We created a whole new category of "network partners." These are people who joined the life of the church all over the country, but will most likely never set foot in our physical building. They come into the digital experience to recite the remixed membership vows we created just for them:

Network Partner Vows

Individuals

Do you want to grow in loving God and neighbor in this community of WildOnes?

- **Prayer:** Will you communicate with God every day?
- **Presence:** Will you join the WildOnes to connect digitally as much as possible?
- **Giving:** Will you give financially as an act of worship that will bless those that are hungry, thirsty, naked, incarcerated, sick, and lonely?
- **Serving:** Will you give your time to love and serve others?
- **Instigating:** Will you stir up kingdom mischief in the name and power of Jesus?

Community

Church, will you surround these persons with a community of love and forgiveness, as they stir up kingdom trouble across the land? (Please type "yes" in the comments section.)

I now pronounce you WildOnes! (Please show your appreciation with likes, loves, and appropriate emojis!)

In the conversational space, we don't try to offer something that is universally prescriptive—only stories, ideas, and principles that could potentially be applied to your own context.

App It

Chat Box

Gather with your team physically or digitally and discuss the following questions.

1. Do a time usage survey on your worship experience. How long is the service? What percentage of your worship experience is spent on liturgy, prayers, music, sermon, offering, sacraments, and so on?

2. When you are experiencing something online, do you find it more or less engaging than in-person?

3. What do you think about Jesus's dialogical style of preaching and his method of asking questions?

4. Read your favorite Jesus story together. Let each person on the team come up with a couple questions designed to spark conversation around the story. What questions would each of you ask? Why?

5. Why do you think a "sermonic conversation" is more accessible to not-yet-Christians or no-longer-Christians? With everything we've learned about technology so far, why do we need to make this shift to more effectively engage our hearers?

6. Choose one of Steve Jobs's presentations for Apple (simply go to YouTube and type into the search bar "Steve Jobs presentations,"

and pick one that looks interesting). What do you notice about Jobs's presentation? How did he use technology, story, and share the stage?

E-haviors

Consider how these practices might be helpful as missionaries in the digital age.

1. **Live, not pre-recorded:** It's very hard to make something interactive and conversational when it's pre-recorded.

2. **Multiple streams:** Stream to multiple platforms at once: Facebook, YouTube, Instagram, your church website, and so on. Engage people on the platforms that make up their digital neighborhood.

3. **Team based (digital ministers):** Have people prepared to engage others in the live service, saying hello, asking questions, and responding to comments.

4. **Steve Jobs style (story, simple, unscripted):** Study how Jobs used technology in his presentations. Harvest learnings from his approach.

5. **TED Talk Rule:** Sermons should not exceed eighteen minutes in a digital medium.

6. **Change screens every three to five minutes:** There is a science to keeping people engaged for an extended period; switching up the screen with purposeful shifts and sharing the stage are important.

7. **Invitational (multiple engagement points):** Always be offering attendees the next level of relationship, opt in experiences, digital "home visits," digital "meet and greet" after gatherings, and so on.

8. **Capture visitors' contact:** Invite attendees to give you their contact information in creative ways. Offer your contact information to them frequently.

9. **Follow up with visitors:** When people give their contact information or indicate interest, follow up quickly.

10. **Redefine "membership":** In the digital ecology, many of your regulars may never set foot in your physical sanctuary. How can

you bring them into the community, welcome them, offer them an opportunity to commit?

11. **Create opportunities for feedback (e.g., use SurveyMonkey, which is free):** Your team is not the best judge of how you are doing in digital worship. Give regular opportunities for feedback from all participants.

Livestream: Ross Stackhouse

I'm Ross Stackhouse. I've been married for ten years to Angela. We have two young kids.

I've been in full-time ministry in The United Methodist Church since 2012, and as a pastor since 2014 (ordained in 2020). I feel called to those who are disconnected or alienated from church community. I also feel called to recover some of the ancient beliefs and practices of the earliest Jesus movements.

In 2018, I was appointed to plant a church south of Indianapolis, Indiana, in the towns of Bargersville, Whiteland, and their surrounding areas. These towns are a mixture of significant progress and a lot of pain. Bargersville has the highest household income in the county and houses one of the highest percentages of families living below the poverty line. Whiteland is also experiencing tremendous growth; however, almost 50 percent of students in the district receive free or reduced lunch at school. One of the greatest challenges the county faces is young adults (ages sixteen to twenty-five) struggling with homelessness.

According to MissionInsite, the greatest increase in religious affiliation in the last ten years in the county is among those who consider themselves "not religious." As I practiced deep listening with dozens of people, I realized that statistics can't demonstrate the intense feelings and heartbreaking stories of people who have left church or, more accurately, of those who feel as if the church has left them.

Meeting people where they are was the first value we adopted as a church. We knew we had to put the incarnation into practice. One way God led us to do this was by forming a partnership with a local barbecue restaurant. We hosted trivia nights on the slowest night of the week. We invited a local nonprofit to share what it was doing, and the restaurant agreed to do a dine-to-donate for the nonprofit. Eventually, we began having Sunday breakfasts in the restaurant.

Meeting people where they are applies to our digital presence as well. I have to be willing to go live on Facebook at any time when the Spirit moves—unscripted and authentic—to share a short story about how I'm witnessing God at work in the community. I once livestreamed at a Kroger grocery store, where I visit frequently to shine light on the people I meet there. I called it the "First Church of Kroger."

We were scheduled to launch weekly Sunday gatherings on Easter of 2020. When COVID-19 hit, our leadership team realized that wasn't going to happen. So, we decided to launch earlier—from my basement.

Sunday mornings have become "Sunday Conversations," where we facilitate more of a dialogue with questions and comments rather than broadcasting a scripted worship service. It's easy to fall back into the "build it and they will come" mindset even with what we do online. We're letting the Spirit lead us to be missional as a way of life, including with what we do online.

LOGOUT

A Missional Posture of Placefulness

In *How to Do Nothing: Resisting the Attention Economy,* Jenny Odell writes:

> My argument is anticapitalist, especially concerning technologies that encourage a capitalist perception of time, place, self, and community. It is also environmental and historical: I propose that rerouting and deepening one's attention to place will likely lead to awareness of one's participation in history and in a more-than-human community. From either a social or ecological perspective, the ultimate goal of "doing nothing" is to wrest our focus from the attention economy and replant it in the public, physical realm.[1]

As we suggested at the beginning, to be missionaries in the space of flows in the digital age, we need to have both feet planted firmly in the analog world. Many of our e-havior suggestions are an attempt to balance engaging the technosphere for its redemption, as well as a *missional posture of placefulness.*

In the network society, "de-territorial-ization" describes the disconnection from geography in a digital world. As we live in the space of real virtuality, hyperconnected by the screens of our technological devices, we become dislocated from our neighborhoods.

152

The COVID-19 pandemic caused us to hunker down and practice social distancing, but simultaneously it forced us to stay in our "place." In many cases we had forgotten that physical space was even there, but exhaustion from the constant fixation on our anxiety-inducing screens, caused us to take walks, look around, see our place again.

Incarnation is all about "placefulness." Jenny Odell employs this term to describe sensitivity and responsibility to the historical (what happened here) and ecological (who and what lives or lived here). Odell holds up bioregionalism (this involves the interrelation of human activity with ecological and geographical features) as a model for how we might be able to think about our place again.

Hopefully we have made a case for seeing digital space as its own kind of "third place," where real community can indeed form. We think this must be held in balance with being in mission to the flesh and blood people that share our zip code. It is possible to resist a capitalist value system, one in which we are completely enmeshed, while also seeking to be a transfiguring agent within it. Like the "yeast" that "had worked its way through the whole" loaf (Luke 13:21).

We do indeed need to take time away to disengage from the attention economy, to enjoy a technological sabbath, and to breathe in the air of our plants, insects, and the critters who share our ecosystem. The essential skills of the modern digital missionary include paying attention to our physical context, understanding its history, knowing where it came from, and wondering where it is going. Leonard Sweet and I call this "contextual intelligence."

Yet the digital reality created by chips, wires, and boards is a context in itself that must be engaged. The Holy Spirit goes before us there too. There are real people living in those spaces, and the only way to be with them will be through their screens and one day their Virtual Reality helmets, goggles, and brain chips. Therefore, a digital missionary must first make the journey to understand the context and implication for our own wellbeing. What are the core wounds? What forces shape us? How does our personality orient toward achievement? These are forces we must pay careful attention to. We can't truly listen to others unless we understand the voice of the Spirit that speaks in us.

Total withdrawal from the online ecosystem is impossible for most disciples who want to be faithful and fruitful to Jesus in the digital age. As Odell writes, "Some hybrid reaction is needed. We have to be able to do both: to contemplate and participate, to leave and always come back, where we are needed."[2] For Odell,

> Civil disobedience in the attention economy means withdrawing attention. . . . A real withdrawal of attention happens first and foremost in the mind. What is needed, then, is not a "once-and-for-all" type of quitting but ongoing training: the ability not just to withdraw attention, but to invest it somewhere else, to enlarge and proliferate its acuity. . . . I am less interested in a mass exodus from Facebook and Twitter than I am in a mass movement of attention: what happens when people regain control of their attention and begin to direct it again, together.[3]

The word *attention* comes from the Latin word *attendere,* from which "to attend" originates; the original Latin denotes "to stretch toward." To give attention requires an element of effort and straining. In the digital age, what we pay attention to is monetized. It is the skill of focusing our attention that will become the most significant on the digital frontier. Those who can give sustained attention to context and from those observations develop appropriate missional behaviors will be able to adapt to whatever changes may come.

The danger for many Christians is being largely unaware about how these technological systems mine our attention for a profit. We become fixated on our screens, and our days are drained away from having any real impact in life. We accept the superficial level of personification dictated by our social media profiles: name, job, schooling, married to, and profile pictures. We must understand that these are not real appropriations of our humanity, but at the same time know that real humans are on the other side of these digital projections.

We have used these technologies to plant real churches with real people, both in the analog and digital spaces. However, these can't be our only missional approach. We need to spend time doing deep listening in the community where we live, work, and play. This will become increasingly important for local churches. The probability of our congregation ever going back to normal is unlikely.

Many people who attended our churches will never return in-person. Some have health issues that will limit embodied participation for years to come; others have found fulfillment in the digital worship gatherings, in some cases at another address. Some will walk away from the faith because they disagreed with how churches managed the pandemic or because they decided they don't need faith at all. This new scenario requires a missional posture of *placefulness* more than ever before.

The key principle driving Fresh Expressions has always been its own form of bioregionalism, understanding the congregation as a habitat within a larger communal ecosystem. The fresh-expressions way is about forming new Christian communities in the rhythms and spaces where people already do life. Christian community is forming at the tavern, tattoo parlor, dog park, running track, skating rink, city park, coffee shop, or hair salon. Part of the power of this blended-ecology is in spreading the church's life out across the whole ecosystem. Every space in the community is a potential church or sacred space and every follower of Jesus a potential pioneer.

As all the people of God are released in their unique giftedness through social networks, the fellowship grows with people who would never darken the door of a church on Sunday mornings. The key to this idea is that smaller gatherings in public spaces make the church more accessible to all people.

This compression allows churches to relax into a posture of "placefulness" in a new way. The church isn't limited to the real estate it owns but is growing and spreading across the community like a mustard seed growing all through the emperor's garden (Matt 13:31-32). For too long in the "Christendom paradigm," we limited our imaginations to what the church can be or do by conflating it to what can happen in the formal religious compound.

This was not the approach taken by Jesus, who spent much time connecting with people throughout the highways and byways where they were already gathering for life.

We draw from the traditions throughout church history, such as the Anabaptists, the wandering missionaries who sought to convert those whom they saw as Christian in name only. We can draw upon the Celtic Christian tradition to root our mission deeply in the environment where we live. This opens up new possibilities for creation care, planting gardens, and social activism on behalf of nature, which is more than just sending money to agencies. We start to see the value and fragmentation of our own environments, and release people to work together with community leaders for the renewal of our communities.

Cities become massively polluted and unsustainable. If we assume a posture of placefulness, we can entertain questions about how the cityscape may be stripped of pollution and renewed through green spaces and implementing green technologies.

Urban environmentalism is an essential area into which God is calling followers of Jesus to get involved. Since the 1950s the population of human beings living in cities has risen six-fold. By 2050 it is projected that almost 70 percent of the world population will live in cities. With the rise in urbanization, the health of the planet is inextricably linked with the future of cities. Churches can be involved in the conversation and activism around economic, social, and environmental aspects of urban design. Most urban renewal projects seem to follow two major patterns: strategies to retrofit existing cities with green technology and entire cities, like Masdar City for instance, which was designed from the start for sustainability and low environmental impact, powered by renewable energy.[4] (Masdar City is in Abu Dhabi, the United Arab Emirates.)

What can the church learn from an eco-city in a desert? Over the course of four decades, a prominent green consciousness has arisen. Some of the brightest minds in the world today are focused on creating *eco-cities*. The current trajectory of human civilization is not sustainable with this increased population growth and continued increase in urbanization. Cities drain 70 percent of global energy resources and emit 80 percent of greenhouse gases. Leading scholars in the field suggest that eco-cities are a key in solving environmental problems and creating a sustainable future. There are currently urban projects on each continent.[5]

The Masdar City project was launched in 2006, and in some ways is a revolutionary prototype of future eco-cities. It is the first of its kind in moving toward a master-planned, zero-carbon, sustainable settlement. Currently, Masdar City is being used as a model of sustainability and urban planning for other eco-city projects. While the city is still under construction, the hub is complete, and around a hundred citizens already call it home. Thus imagination, innovation, technology, and architecture have fused together to create an incarnate eco-city that can be studied as a kind of living laboratory.[6]

While the project has experienced significant adversity, including loss of some of the initial financial backing, the vision was to create the world's first zero-waste, zero-carbon settlement that produced no adverse environmental impact. Using cutting-edge architecture and green technology, the city was designed to use smart utility grids, concentrated solar power, and electric personal rapid transport.

Federico Cugurullo, a professor in Smart and Sustainable Urbanism at Trinity College Dublin, wrote an article titled "How to Build a Sandcastle: An Analysis of the Genesis and Development of Masdar City" in which he evaluates the project on what he identifies as the "triple bottom line" of economic, social, and environmental sustainability. In pulling together significant data, he finds Masdar City to be lacking in each of these three dimensions. Unfortunately, at the end of the day, the project is a capitalist venture driven by profits. The data on the environmental impact is not solid and the economic model is yet to be determined. In the social realm, Masdar City is little more than a handful of profiteers and scientists.[7]

While setbacks and complications have delayed the project, and designers were forced to make concessions to the original plan, Masdar City is truly a wonder of the postmodern world and is a glimpse of the future of urban life. For our purposes, we want to employ Masdar City as an "imaginarium" through which to approach the blended-ecology way. Let's use the three lenses of eco-city development—economic, social, and environmental—to discuss the dimensions of local church ecosystems. Most churches in decline focus on one of those dimensions, economic, and tend to view the social as confined to the existing congregation only. We need to refocus on the environment, and the larger social networks of the community where the church is positioned.

It's our hope that this adventure in digital fresh expressions will help us break free from the confines of the institutional church and help to steer us free from the cul-de-sac of church fights and property disputes. Chances are good that you are fully aware that the current institutional church systems are no longer sustainable. We don't need to keep creating churches or recreating them in the same old way. That is a dead end. If you are involved in planting a church or an ambitious fresh expression, spend some time studying Masdar City. We can design new churches with the eco-city in mind.

Masdar City could be understood as a type of blended ecology, where inherited systems like architecture, community, and construction are reconfigured around a certain missional focus. In the case of Masdar City, the missional focus is creating a sustainable city that doesn't depend on current energy sources or pollute the environment. Thus, the design is reimagined and transformed by engaging the newest green technologies. The inherited systems and the emerging innovations are blended and reconfigured to create new structures. This enables a different kind of community, an overall healthier ecosystem, and a sustainable future.

Within this framework, imagine the kind of ecclesiological remix the shifting missional frontier requires. Inherited churches, like existing cities, were not designed for sustainability or eco-friendliness. The ecclesiological systems and the real properties of local churches were designed for a world that no longer exists. The assumptions those systems were built upon are no longer valid. Most churches were built in a Christendom context where most of the population attended a parish in a geographical neighborhood. Just like cities were built during thriving boom periods, so denominational systems were wired into a boom.

With little foresight or ecological concern, cities were constructed to accommodate population growth and urbanization. Cities not only pollute the ecosystem, they also negatively impact the health of the residents. Repurposing vacant lots and dilapidated neighborhoods as green spaces has emerged as a response to these realities. Denominations also capitalized on population growth and urbanization with little regard to future implications. Now massive, clunky systems put the pressure on local congregations to make up for declining resources. Smaller groups of people in churches are supporting systems that have remained largely the same.

Regarding actual properties, functionally speaking, church facilities may be one of the least efficacious uses of building and space imaginable. Spacious sanctuaries, designed to accommodate growing congregations now are sparsely populated on Sunday mornings. Church buildings largely sit empty throughout the week. Some facilities, in poverty-stricken neighborhoods where homelessness is a real epidemic are only used for a couple hours on Sunday mornings. Signs that warn against trespassers, such as "no skateboarding" or "no playing" cause neighborhood youth to see the church as some odd, angry relic of an age past.

In many parts of the United States and Europe, the critical challenge leans more toward dealing with aging building materials and unsustainable urban infrastructure. Across the United States, a new breed of urban engineers is employing imagination, creativity, and innovative technologies to retrofit existing cities. They are discovering that, through retrofitting, the potential of cities may also provide their solutions.

Retrofitting existing cities is the greatest challenge to healing our ecosystem and enabling human thriving in the future. We need some of our best and brightest minds working on the remixing of neighborhoods in a sustainable way and creating green space. Technology is being employed in positive ways to affect these changes. In a world that is beginning to design eco-cities, it's time for us to design some eco-churches.

The church plays a significant role in the complex networks within the ecosystem. It's like a green space within that network. It provides the life-giving oxygen that helps the community breathe and heal from isolation.

It's a haven, an oasis, for the 24/7 work-anxiety cycle of our world. In most cases, the people in our communities have become habituated to living in the unsustainable cycles of pollution and sin. They are largely unaware of the need to recreate the community in a sustainable way, so we will need to open the imaginations of our community to this reality.

Recovering a missional posture of placefulness is essential to begin this work of renewing the planet we have plundered mercilessly throughout the Industrial Age. A choice between placefulness and incarnational mission on the digital frontier is a false dichotomy. Every believer can faithfully engage both the neighborhood and the online global village that grows each day.

App It

Chat Box

Gather with your team physically or digitally and discuss the following questions.

1. In what ways did Jesus assume a "posture of placefulness"? How did he teach his disciples to do this? Think of some specific examples in scripture.

2. Can you describe your context using all five senses? Share these with each other.

3. In the midst of cultivating new Christian communities in the digital space, how are you grounding yourself in the physical space?

4. What practices do you use to resist falling prey to the "attention economy"? How are you engaging the digital space without being consumed by it?

5. How many walks a day do you take? What do you notice mostly when you do?

6. What are the greatest needs and challenges in your zip code? Do you love your place enough to weep over it?

E-haviors

Consider how these practices might be helpful as missionaries in the digital age.

1. **Deep work:** Cal Newport has written the amazing book, *Deep Work: Rules for Focused Success in a Distracted World.* When we entertain distractions, they disrupt our capacity for deep, complex thinking. Residual attention clings to the distraction when we engage. Schedule times to minimize all technological distractions to focus on complex, meaningful tasks (preparing sermons, lesson planning, writing books, etc.).[8]

2. **Take walks:** Some of the greatest ideas in human history came through walks. Some of the most brilliant thinkers in history were known for taking frequent walks. Go outside, breath in the air, walk and decompress.

3. **Pay attention to the physical environment:** While some walks should be mindless moments of flow, another great practice is paying careful attention to the physical ecosystem around you. What grows here? What critters are running loose? Who are my neighbors? What are the smells and colors of this place?

4. **Stink and sweat every day:** This is one of Michael's favorites. Particularly in the digital age, we need to do some physically exhausting routine. There's loads of brain research to back this up! Exercise improves attention, positive mood, emotional well-being, and so on.[9]

5. **Do some form of non-digital art:** The activities of painting, hand-writing poetry, making pottery, creating origami figures, and so on exercise different muscles in the brain. Getting into a state of flow during these activities helps us strengthen areas of the brain dedicated to attention, areas that diminish through engagement with digital technology.

6. **Never surf and eat:** Another terrible habit that has come along in the digital age is the tendency to be on our screens as we eat. This is a terrible habit that takes us away from being present in the very spiritual act of eating. We mindlessly surf the web, while not appropriately chewing our food. God gave us taste buds to enjoy the many splendorous creations on our tables. The exception to this rule is when we are eating with others in a digital space intentionally.

Livestream:
Djuna Shorter

I'm Djuna Shorter. I've been a worshipper all my life, mostly with a microphone in my hand guiding our congregations into encounters with the Holy Spirit. After stepping down from my last leadership position, I questioned how God was going to use me next. How was I going to continue to grow God's kingdom if not through worship?

Shortly thereafter our world was facing the onset of a global pandemic and surprisingly, through the chaos, God made it very clear what I was supposed to be doing. I currently serve as the Online Worship Director for Mosaic Church in Dayton, Ohio, and I also coordinate and produce online worship for the chapels of Wright Patterson Air Force Base (WPAFB).

These are two very different audiences, but Jesus is still the same. Broadcasting a worship experience each week has been an incredible way to engage people beyond my physical reach, to bring Jesus into their homes, for them to encounter God's presence at their own pace.

Through Mosaic's online worship experience, we've been able to cultivate relationships with people from Hawaii to Africa. We've also been able to attract a broader audience by incorporating different cultures and languages into our worship experience each week.

Soon we aim to broadcast our service in Spanish as well as English. It's important for us not only to represent all God's kingdom during in-person worship but also in our online expressions as well.

Through WPAFB Chapels, we've been able to reach airmen who were not able to attend regular worship services because they were on duty. Both are tremendous examples of God's kingdom on earth.

Notes

Login

1. For an in-depth treatment of Fresh Expressions see, Michael Beck with Jorge Acevedo, *A Field Guide to Methodist Fresh Expressions* (Nashville: Abingdon Press, 2020).

2. David Sax, *The Revenge of Analog: Real Things and Why They Matter* (New York: PublicAffairs, 2017), 10.

Download 1: The Digital Age

1. Manuel Castells, *The Rise of the Network Society* (Oxford and Malden, MA: Blackwell, 2000), xxxi.

2. Ralph Waldo Emerson, "The Young American," in *The Collected Works of Ralph Waldo Emerson*, vol. I: Nature, Addresses, and Lectures, ed. Robert E. Spiller (Cambridge, MA: Belknap, 1971), 230.

3. Quoted in Daniel W. Howe, *What Hath God Wrought: The Transformation of America, 1815–1848* (New York: Oxford University Press, 2007), 23.

4. Howe, *What Hath God Wrought*, 15.

5. Quoted in Howe, *What Hath God Wrought*, 24.

6. Jacques Ellul, Ted Lewis, and Lisa Richmond, *Presence in the Modern World: A New Translation* (Eugene: Wipf and Stock Publishers, 2016), 19.

7. Ellul, Lewis, and Richmond, *Presence in the Modern World*, 58.

8. Ellul, Lewis, and Richmond, *Presence in the Modern World*, 63.

9. Ellul, Lewis, and Richmond, *Presence in the Modern World*, 50.

10. Marshall McLuhan, and W. T. Gordon, *Understanding Media: The Extensions of Man* (Corte Madera, CA: Gingko, 2003), 9.

11. Marshall McLuhan, *The Gutenberg Galaxy: The Making of Typographic Man* (Toronto: University of Toronto Press, 2011), 76.

12. McLuhan, *Gutenberg*, 118.

13. Brad Smith and Carol A. Browne, *Tools and Weapons: The Promise and the Peril of the Digital Age* (New York: Penguin, 2019), 85.

14. Smith and Browne, *Tools and Weapons*, 85.

15. Jimmy Soni and Rob Goodman, *A Mind at Play: How Claude Shannon Invented the Information Age* (New York: Simon & Schuster, 2017).

16. John Dyer, *From the Garden to the City: The Redeeming and Corrupting Power of Technology* (Grand Rapids: Kregel, 2011), 67.

17. Data provided from Abingdon Press hymnal research in August 2019.

18. Kevin Kelly, *The Inevitable: Understanding the 12 Technological Forces That Will Shape Our Future* (New York: Penguin, 2017), 135–43.

19. Marilee Sprenger, *Brain-Based Teaching in the Digital Age* (Alexandria, VA: Association for Supervision and Curriculum Development, 2010), xiii.

20. Jenny Odell, *How to Do Nothing: Resisting the Attention Economy* (Brooklyn: Melville House, 2019), xi.

21. For more, see Susan Greenfield, *Mind Change: How Digital Technologies Are Leaving Their Mark on Our Brains* (New York: Random House, 2015).

22. McLuhan, *Gutenberg*, 249.

23. Sprenger, *Brain-Based Teaching*, 7, 14, and 3.

24. Smith and Browne, *Tools and Weapons*, 10.

25. Dyer, *From the Garden to the City*, 28.

26. Manuel Castells, *The Rise of the Network Society* (Oxford and Malden, MA: Blackwell, 2000), xvii–xviii.

27. Castells, *The Rise of the Network Society*, xxxi.

28. Castells, *The Rise of the Network Society*, xxxi.

29. Castells, *The Rise of the Network Society*, 442.

30. Castells, *The Rise of the Network Society*, xxix.

31. Timothy W. Luke, "Cyberspace as Meta-Nation: The Net Effects of Online E-Publicanism," *Alternatives: Global, Local, Political*, vol. 26, no. 2 (2001): 113.

32. Luke, "Cyberspace as Meta-Nation," 113.

33. Luke, "Cyberspace as Meta-Nation," 113.

34. See Internet Growth Statistics 1995 to 2019, the Global Village Online https://www.internetworldstats.com/emarketing.htm, https://www.broadbandsearch.net/blog/internet-statistics, and https://www.statista.com/markets/. Accessed December 15, 2020.

35. Tricia Harte, "Americans Underestimate Daily Screen Time, According to New Study," *Grit Daily*, April 2, 2019, https://gritdaily.com/daily-screen-time/. Accessed December 15, 2020.

36. Sprenger, *Brain-Based Teaching*, xiii.

37. Sprenger, *Brain-Based Teaching*, 12.

Download 2: The COVID-19 Reset

1. *Strong's Greek Concordance:* 1577. κκλησία (ekklésia): an assembly, a (religious) congregation. https://biblehub.com/greek/1577.htm. Accessed May 29, 2020.

2. Wayne Jackson, "What Is the Meaning of Ekklesia?" *ChristianCourier.com*, https://www.christiancourier.com/articles/1500-what-is-the-meaning-of-ekklesia. Accessed May 29, 2020.

3. "Guidelines: Opening Up America," Atlanta: The US Centers for Disease Control and Prevention (CDC), May 22, 2020.

4. "Guidelines: Opening Up America."

5. "Guidelines: Opening Up America."

6. Rosario Picardo, "Pastoral Update," n.d.

7. Michael Beck, weekly email and newsletter blurb.

8. Michael A. Beck, *Deep Roots, Wild Branches: Revitalizing the Church in the Blended Ecology* (Franklin, TN: Seedbed, 2019).

9. "About Us—Embrace Church," Welcome to Embrace, Embrace Church, https://iamembrace.com/about-us. Accessed May 30, 2020.

10. Scott D. Anthony, Clark G. Gilbert, and Mark W. Johnson, *Dual Transformation: How to Reposition Today's Business While Creating the Future* (Harvard Business Review Press, 2017).

11. Anthony, Gilbert, and Johnson, *Dual Transformation*, 17.

12. Anthony, Gilbert, and Johnson, *Dual Transformation*, 44–45.

13. Anthony, Gilbert, and Johnson, *Dual Transformation*, 126.

14. Anthony, Gilbert, and Johnson, *Dual Transformation*, location 603.

Download 3: Hybridity—The Post-Pandemic Church

1. Michael has written an entire book anchored in this metaphor. See Michael Beck, *Deep and Wild: Remissioning Your Church from the Outside In* (Franklin, TN: Seedbed, 2020).

2. https://www.samvanaken.com/tree-of-40-fruit-1/. Accessed December 22, 2020.

3. Rachel McRady, "Jimmy Fallon's Kids Hilariously Interrupt His Monologue," *Entertainment Tonight*, March 25, 2020, https://www.etonline.com/jimmy-fallons -kids-hilariously-interrupt-his-monologue-and-working-parents-can-relate-143612. Accessed December 15, 2020.

4. Nathan Bomey, "Can These 13 Retailers Survive Coronavirus? Permanent Store Closings, Bankruptcies Coming," *USA Today* (Gannett Satellite Information Network, May 10, 2020), https://www.usatoday.com/story/money/2020/05/08 /store-closings-chapter-11-bankruptcy-coronavirus-covid-19/3090235001/. Accessed December 15, 2020.

5. Rosario Picardo, "Mission & Vision," Mosaic Church—Mission and Vision, January 1, 2017, https://wearemosaic.org/mission-and-vision. Accessed December 15, 2020.

6. Andrew Van Dam and Heather Long, "U.S. Unemployment Rate Soars to 14.7 Percent, the Worst since the Depression Era," *The Washington Post* (WP Company, May 8, 2020), https://www.washingtonpost.com/business/2020/05/08/april-2020-jobs-report/.

Download 4: Digital Worship—Liturgy, Lectionary, and Utilizing Free-Tech

1. See John S. McClure, *The Roundtable Pulpit: Where Leadership and Preaching Meet* (Nashville: Abingdon Press, 1995) and Ronald A. Allen, *The Sermon Without End: A Conversational Approach to Preaching* (Nashville: Abingdon Press, 2015).

2. See John Voelz, *Follow You/Follow Me: Why Social Networking Is Essential to Ministry* (Nashville: Abingdon Press, 2012).

Download 5: Digital Incarnation—Rethinking Evangelism and Discipleship

1. John M. Foley, *Oral Tradition and the Internet: Pathways of the Mind* (Urbana: University of Illinois Press, 2012).

2. Andrew Martindale, Sara Shneiderman, and Mark Turin, "Time, Oral Tradition, and Technology," *Memory*, ed. Philippe Tortelle, et al. (Vancouver, BC: Peter Wall Institute for Advanced Studies, 2018), 197–206. http://www.jstor.org/stable/j.ctvbtzpfm.26. Accessed December 15, 2020.

3. Martindale, Shneiderman, and Turin, "Time, Oral Tradition, and Technology," 204

4. Martindale, Shneiderman, and Turin, "Time, Oral Tradition, and Technology," 204.

5. Martindale, Shneiderman, and Turin, "Time, Oral Tradition, and Technology," 202.

6. Martindale, Shneiderman, and Turin, "Time, Oral Tradition, and Technology," 202.

7. McLuhan, *The Gutenberg Galaxy*, 252.

8. Leonard Sweet, "Preaching in a Pandemic World," https://www.facebook.com/lensweet/videos/10156741846241791/. Accessed December 15, 2020.

9. Albert R. Jonsen, *A Short History of Medical Ethics* (New York: Oxford University Press, 2000).

10. Steve Hollinghurst, *Mission-Shaped Evangelism: The Gospel in Contemporary Culture* (Norwich, UK: Canterbury, 2010), 208.

11. Alicia Keys, "Good Job," https://youtu.be/gmzUMgyOvBo.

12. Paul Althaus, *The Theology of Martin Luther* (Philadelphia: Fortress, 1970), 328.

13. Rahul Sharma, Sapir Nachum, Karina W. Davidson, and Michael Nochomovitz, "It's Not Just Facetime: Core Competencies for the Medical Virtualist," *International Journal of Emergency Medicine*, vol. 12, no. 1 (2019): 1–5.

14. Sharma, et al., "It's Not Just Facetime," 1–5.

15. Elias Aboujaoude, Wael Salame, and Lama Naim, "Telemental Health: A Status Update," *World Psychiatry*, vol. 14, no. 2 (2015): 223–30. doi:10.1002/wps.20218. https://onlinelibrary.wiley.com/doi/full/10.1002/wps.20218.

16. Aboujaoude, Salame, and Naim, "Telemental Health," 223–30.

17. John Dyer, *From the Garden to the City: The Redeeming and Corrupting Power of Technology* (Grand Rapids: Kregel, 2011), 34.

18. Vincent J. Donovan, *Christianity Rediscovered* (Maryknoll, NY: Orbis, 2003), xiii.

19. See Origen, *Homilies on Luke, 22, 3*, trans. Joseph T. Lienhard (Washington DC: The Catholic University Press of America, 1996), 94: "For what profit is it to you, if Christ came once in the flesh, unless he also comes into your soul?"

20. Quoted in Dyer, *From the Garden to the City*, 130.

21. Dyer, *From the Garden to the City*, 130.

22. Wesley's journal entry, dated August 25, 1763.

23. Jack Jackson, *Offering Christ: John Wesley's Evangelistic Vision* (Nashville: Kingswood, 2017), 146.

24. Jackson, *Offering Christ*, 155.

25. Jackson, *Offering Christ*, 158.

26. Jackson, *Offering Christ*, 181.

27. Hollinghurst, *Mission-Shaped Evangelism*, 242.

Download 6: Cultivating Digital Fresh Expressions

1. David W. Augsburger, *Caring Enough to Hear and Be Heard* (Ventura, CA: Regal, 1982).

2. Sherry Turkle, *Alone Together: Why We Expect More from Technology and Less from Each Other* (New York: Basic, 2017), 238.

3. Turkle, *Alone Together*, 239.

4. Michael Adam Beck, "A Missional Meal: The Digital Practice of the Lord's Supper," *Ministry Matters*, April 14, 2020, https://www.ministrymatters.com/all /entry/10274/a-missional-meal-the-digital-practice-of-the-lords-supper. Accessed December 15, 2020.

5. Nadia Drake, "Elon Musk: A Million Humans Could Live on Mars By the 2060s," *National Geographic*, September 27, 2016, https://www.nationalgeographic .com/news/2016/09/elon-musk-spacex-exploring-mars-planets-space-science/. Accessed December 15, 2020.

Download 7: Going Old-School in a New-School World

1. Lee Siegel, "Why Is America So Depressed?" *The New York Times*, January 2, 2020, https://www.nytimes.com/2020/01/02/opinion/depression-america-trump .html.

2. Caroline Miller, "Does Social Media Cause Depression?" *Child Mind Institute*, June 11, 2020, https://childmind.org/article/is-social-media-use-causing -depression/.

3. Gigen Mammoser, "Social Media Increases Depression and Loneliness," *Healthline*, December 10, 2018, https://www.healthline.com/health-news/social -media-use-increases-depression-and-loneliness.

4. David Roach, "Bible Reading Drops During Social Distancing," News & Reporting, *Christianity Today*, July 22, 2020, https://www.christianitytoday.com /news/2020/july/state-of-bible-reading-coronavirus-barna-abs.html.

5. Allen Hirsch, "Media," What is APEST?, n.d., *The Forgotten Ways*, https://www.theforgottenways.org/what-is-apest.aspx. Accessed December 15, 2020.

6. Ananhad O'Connor, "How to Get Strong," *The New York Times*, https://www.nytimes.com/guides/year-of-living-better/how-to-build-muscle-strength. Accessed December 15, 2020.

7. Frances Borsodi Zajac, "Belle Vernon Church Offers Drive-thru Prayer," *Herald Standard*, March 29, 2020, https://www.heraldstandard.com/news/covid-19/belle-vernon-church-offers-drive-thru-prayer/article_15b0ba20-703f-11ea-bf77-f7c93eb14bb1.html. Accessed December 15, 2020.

8. Kelsey Dickeson, "Minden Church Hosts Drive-thru Communion, Will Continue Social Distancing Measures through May," Local KSNB Hastings, May 4, 2020, https://www.ksnblocal4.com/content/news/Minden-church-hosts-drive-thru-communion-will-continue-social-distancing-measures-through-May-570161321.html. Accessed December 15, 2020.

9. Stephen B. Bevans and Roger Schroeder, *Prophetic Dialogue: Reflections on Christian Mission Today* (Maryknoll, NY: Orbis, 2011), 15.

10. Eugene H. Peterson, "John," *The Message: The Bible in Contemporary Language* (Colorado Springs: NavPress, 2006).

Download 8: From Monologues to Dialogues

1. Nicholas Carr, *The Shallows: What the Internet Is Doing to Our Brains* (New York: W. W. Norton, 2020), 20.

2. In other words, this engagement is a form of what Wesley meant by holy conversation—rather than classical preaching as rhetoric. In the nineteenth century on the frontier, the Methodist and Baptist circuit riders often began by planting Sunday schools, which preceded the formation of institutional congregations. The "Sunday-school movement" in America persisted until the 1970s, when it began a slow decline. To this day, thousands of older-adult Sunday morning classes function as mini-churches, including singing, prayer, witness, missional service, and a dated lesson.

3. C. H. Dodd, *The Apostolic Preaching and Its Developments* (New York: Harper & Row, 1964), 7.

4. Dodd, *Apostolic Preaching*, 23

5. Herman Horne, *Jesus, The Master Teacher* (Miami: HardPress, 2012), 11.

6. Horne, *Jesus, The Master Teacher*, 12.

7. Horne, *Jesus, The Master Teacher*, 13.

8. Martin Copenhaver, *Jesus Is the Question: The 307 Questions Jesus Asked and the 3 He Answered* (Nashville: Abingdon Press, 2014), xix, 71.

9. James Rodney Briggs, "The Development and Testing of a Curriculum for Inquiry-Based Leadership in the Ecclesia Network for the Advancement of God's Mission" (thesis dissertation, 2019), 39. See https://rim.atla.com/index.php/node/37210 for full text. Accessed December 15, 2020.

10. Briggs, "The Development and Testing of a Curriculum for Inquiry-Based Leadership," 39.

11. Carmine Gallo, *The Presentation Secrets of Steve Jobs: How to Be Insanely Great in Front of Any Audience* (New York: McGraw-Hill Education, 2016), 129.

12. Gallo, *The Presentation Secrets of Steve Jobs*, 129.

Logout: A Missional Posture of Placefulness

1. Jenny Odell, *How to Do Nothing: Resisting the Attention Economy* (Brooklyn: Melville House, 2019), xii.

2. Odell, *How to Do Nothing*, 61.

3. Odell, *How to Do Nothing*, 92–93.

4. You can watch the Sustainable City | Fully Charged documentary on Masdar City on YouTube: https://www.youtube.com/watch?v=WCKz8ykyI2E&t=630s. Accessed December 15, 2020.

5. Federico Cugurullo, "How to Build a Sandcastle: An Analysis of the Genesis and Development of Masdar City," *Journal of Urban Technology*, vol. 20, no. 1 (2013): 23–37, p. 24.

6. Cugurullo, "How to Build a Sandcastle," 26.

7. Cugurullo, "How to Build a Sandcastle," 26.

8. Cal Newport, *Deep Work: Rules for Focused Success in a Distracted World* (New York: Grand Central, 2016).

9. Marilee Sprenger, *Brain-Based Teaching in the Digital Age* (Alexandria, VA: Association for Supervision and Curriculum Development, 2010), 21–22.

References

Aboujaoude, Elias, Wael Salame, and Lama Naim. "Telemental Health: A Status Update." *World Psychiatry*, vol. 14, no. 2 (2015): 223–30.

Anthony, Scott D., Clark G. Gilbert, and Mark W. Johnson. *Dual Transformation: How to Reposition Today's Business While Creating the Future*, 2017.

Beck, Michael, with Jorge Acevedo. *A Field Guide to Methodist Fresh Expressions*. Nashville: Abingdon Press, 2020.

Beck, Michael A. *Deep Roots, Wild Branches: Revitalizing the Church in the Blended Ecology*. Franklin, TN: Seedbed, 2019.

———. *Deep and Wild: Remissioning Your Church from the Outside In*. Franklin, TN: Seedbed, 2021 (in press).

———. https://www.ministrymatters.com/all/entry/10274/a-missional-meal-the -digital-practice-of-the-lords-supper.

Bomey, Nathan. "Can These 13 Retailers Survive Coronavirus? Permanent Store Closings, Bankruptcies Coming," *USA Today* (Gannett Satellite Information Network, May 10, 2020), https://www.usatoday.com/story/money/2020/05/08 /store-closings-chapter-11-bankruptcy-coronavirus-covid-19/3090235001/.

Borsodi, Frances. "Belle Vernon Church Offers Drive-thru Prayer," heraldstandard .com, March 29, 2020, https://www.heraldstandard.com/news/covid-19 /belle-vernon-church-offers-drive-thru-prayer/article_15b0ba20-703f-11ea -bf77-f7c93eb14bb1.html.

Briggs, James Rodney (J. R.). "The Development and Testing of a Curriculum for Inquiry-Based Leadership in the Ecclesia Network for the Advancement of God's Mission," 2019.

Castells, Manuel. *The Rise of the Network Society*. Oxford and Malden, MA: Blackwell, 2000.

Carr, Nicholas G. *The Shallows: What the Internet Is Doing to Our Brains*. New York: W. W. Norton, 2020.

CDC. "Guidelines: Opening Up America." Atlanta: The US Centers for Disease Control and Prevention, May 22, 2020.

Copenhaver, Martin. *Jesus Is the Question: The 307 Questions Jesus Asked and the 3 He Answered*. Nashville: Abingdon Press, 2014.

Crouch, Andy. *The Tech-Wise Family: Everyday Steps for Putting Technology in Its Proper Place*. Grand Rapids: Baker, 2017.

Cugurullo, Federico. "How to Build a Sandcastle: An Analysis of the Genesis and Development of Masdar City," *Journal of Urban Technology*, vol. 20, no. 1 (2013): 23.

Dickeson, Kelsey. "Minden Church Hosts Drive-thru Communion, Will Continue Social Distancing Measures through May," https://www.ksnblocal4.com, May 3, 2020, https://www.ksnblocal4.com/content/news/Minden-church -hosts-drive-thru-communion-will-continue-social-distancing-measures -through-May-570161321.html.

Drake, Nadia. https://www.nationalgeographic.com/news/2016/09/elon-musk-space x-exploring-mars-planets-space-science/.

Dodd, C. H. *The Apostolic Preaching and Its Developments*. New York and Evanston: Harper & Row, 1964.

Donovan, Vincent J. *Christianity Rediscovered*. Maryknoll, NY: Orbis, 2003.

Dyer, John. *From the Garden to the City: The Redeeming and Corrupting Power of Technology*. Grand Rapids: Kregel, 2011.

Ellul, Jacques, Ted Lewis, and Lisa Richmond. *Presence in the Modern World: A New Translation*. Eugene, OR: Wipf and Stock, 2016.

Fetzer Institute. "Virtual Sacred Space: A Report." https://fetzer.org/sites/default /files/2020-10/Creating%20Sacred%20Space%20Virtually%20FI%20 Report%2009-20.pdf.

Foley, John M. *Oral Tradition and the Internet: Pathways of the Mind*. Urbana: University of Illinois Press, 2012.

Fully Charged. Documentary on Masdar City, "The Sustainable City." YouTube, https://www.youtube.com/watch?v=WCKz8ykyI2E&t=630s.

Gallo, Carmine. *The Presentation Secrets of Steve Jobs: How to Be Insanely Great in Front of Any Audience.* New York: McGraw-Hill Education, 2016.

Greenfield, Susan. *Mind Change: How Digital Technologies Are Leaving Their Mark on Our Brains.* New York: Random House, 2015.

Hirsch, Alan. "MEDIA," What Is APEST?, n.d., https://www.theforgottenways.org /what-is-apest.aspx.

Hollinghurst, Steve. *Mission-Shaped Evangelism: The Gospel in Contemporary Culture.* Norwich, UK: Canterbury, 2010.

Horne, Herman. *Jesus, The Master Teacher.* Miami: HardPress, 1920.

Howe, Daniel W. *What Hath God Wrought: The Transformation of America, 1815– 1848.* New York: Oxford University Press, 2007.

Jackson, Jack. *Offering Christ: John Wesley's Evangelistic Vision.* Nashville: Kingswood, 2017.

Jackson, Wayne. "What Is the Meaning of Ekklesia?" *ChristianCourier.com.* https:// www.christiancourier.com/articles/1500-what-is-the-meaning-of-ekklesia.

Jonsen, Albert R. *A Short History of Medical Ethics.* New York: Oxford University Press, 2000.

Kelly, Kevin. *The Inevitable: Understanding the 12 Technological Forces That Will Shape Our Future.* New York: Penguin, 2017.

Keys, Alicia. "Good Job," https://youtu.be/gmzUMgyOvBo.

Kreider, Alan. *The Patient Ferment of the Early Church: The Improbable Rise of Christianity in the Roman Empire.* Grand Rapids: Baker Academic, 2016.

Luke, Timothy W. "Cyberspace as Meta-Nation: The Net Effects of Online E-Publicanism," *Alternatives: Global, Local, Political*, vol. 26, no. 2, 2001.

Mammoser, Gigen. "The FOMO Is Real: How Social Media Increases Depression and Loneliness," Healthline (Healthline Media, December 10, 2018), https:// www.healthline.com/health-news/social-media-use-increases-depression -and-loneliness.

Martindale, Andrew, Sara Shneiderman, and Mark Turin. "Time, Oral Tradition and Technology" (2018), https://www.researchgate.net/publication/330918376_Time_oral_tradition_and_technology.

McLuhan, Marshall. *The Gutenberg Galaxy: The Making of Typographic Man*. Toronto: University of Toronto Press, 2011.

McLuhan, Marshall, and W. T. Gordon. *Understanding Media: The Extensions of Man*. Corte Madera, CA: Gingko, 2003.

McRady, Rachel. "Jimmy Fallon's Kids Hilariously Interrupt His Monologue," *Entertainment Tonight* (March 26, 2020), https://www.etonline.com/jimmy-fallons-kids-hilariously-interrupt-his-monologue-and-working-parents-can-relate-143612.

Miller, Caroline. "Does Social Media Cause Depression?" *Child Mind Institute*, June 11, 2020, https://childmind.org/article/is-social-media-use-causing-depression/.

Newport, Cal. *Deep Work: Rules for Focused Success in a Distracted World*. New York: Grand Central, 2016.

Odell, Jenny. *How to Do Nothing: Resisting the Attention Economy*. Brooklyn: Melville House, 2019.

O'Connor, Ananhad. "How to Get Strong," *The New York Times*, https://www.nytimes.com/guides/year-of-living-better/how-to-build-muscle-strength.

Peterson, Eugene H. "John," in *The Message: The Bible in Contemporary Language*. NavPress, 2006.

Roach, David. "Bible Reading Drops During Social Distancing," *News & Reporting*, *Christianity Today*, July 22, 2020, https://www.christianitytoday.com/news/2020/july/state-of-bible-reading-coronavirus-barna-abs.html.

Sax, David. *The Revenge of Analog: Real Things and Why They Matter*. New York: PublicAffairs, 2017.

Siegel, Lee. "Why Is America So Depressed?" *The New York Times*, January 2, 2020, https://www.nytimes.com/2020/01/02/opinion/depression-america-trump.html.

Sharma, Rahul, Sapir Nachum, Karina W. Davidson, and Michael Nochomovitz. "It's Not Just Facetime: Core Competencies for the Medical Virtualist." *International Journal of Emergency Medicine*, vol. 12, no. 1 (2019): 1–5.

Smith, Brad, and Carol A. Browne. *Tools and Weapons: The Promise and the Peril of the Digital Age*. New York: Penguin, 2019.

Soni, Jimmy, and Rob Goodman. *A Mind at Play: How Claude Shannon Invented the Information Age*. New York: Simon & Schuster, 2017.

Sprenger, Marilee. *Brain-Based Teaching in the Digital Age*. Alexandria, VA: Association for Supervision and Curriculum Development, 2010.

Sweet, Leonard, and Michael Adam Beck. *Contextual Intelligence: Unlocking the Ancient Secret to Mission on the Front Lines*. Higherlife Development SE, 2021.

Sweet, Leonard. "Preaching in a Pandemic World," https://www.facebook.com/lensweet/videos/10156741846241791/.

Turkle, Sherry. *Alone Together: Why We Expect More from Technology and Less from Each Other*. New York: Basic, 2017.

Van Dam, Andrew, and Heather Long, "U.S. Unemployment Rate Soars to 14.7 Percent, the Worst since the Depression Era," *The Washington Post*, WP Company, May 8, 2020, https://www.washingtonpost.com/business/2020/05/08/april-2020-jobs-report/.

Wesley, John, et al. *The Works of John Wesley*. Nashville: Abingdon Press, 1984.